THE
SERVANT
LEADER'S
MANIFESTO

OMAR L. HARRIS

First published by Intent Books 2020

ISBN: 978-1-7348815-0-9

Library of Congress cataloging-in-publication data is available

First edition

Cover design: Cathi Stevenson BookCoverExpress.com

Design: BeAPurplePenguin.com

Images reproduced with permission: standard licenses stock.adobe.com and depositphotos.com

Manifesto

[man-uh-fes-toh]

noun, plural, man·i·fes·toes
A public declaration of intentions, opinions, objectives, or motives

For Dad,
My first, and still the best, example of servant leadership

For Mom,
For potentializing my talents

For Kobe Bryant,
For your relentless pursuit of excellence

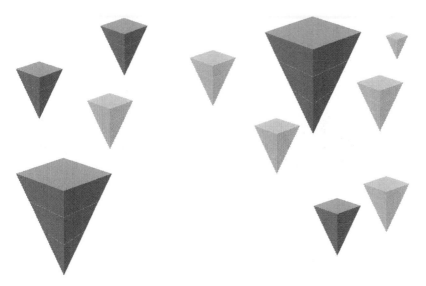

Contents

Introduction · 11

1

What Is Servant Leadership? · 19

2

How to Manifest Personal Effectiveness · 25

3

Use Influence, Not Authority · 33

4

How to Leverage Positive Psychology for Success · 41

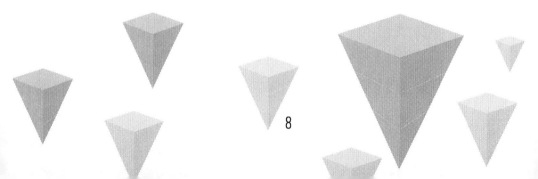

5

Focus on Your Team, Not Individual Talent · 53

6

Perpetuating the Game: From Performance to Progress · 63

7

Lead with Love · 73

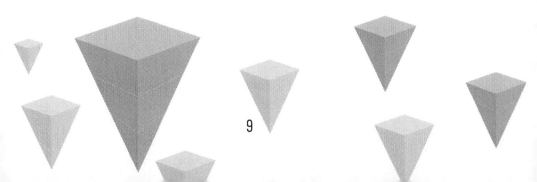

8

The Servant Leader's Learning Journey · 85

References · 93

Afterword · 99

Leader Board: The DNA of High Performance Teams · 103

Foreword: Team DNA · 105

About the Author · 109

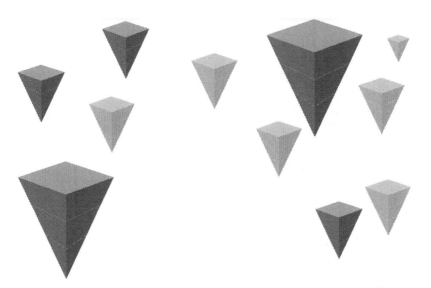

Introduction

Why this matters

Leadership matters. Although the goal has always been to push human progress forward, the methods have not always been in alignment with the times. From the feudal days of indentured servitude to today's information age, the *what* motivating human potential has seen dramatic change, but often the *how* has lagged behind.

The three epochs of leadership

Modern democratic society has progressed through at least three broad epochs in terms of leadership. There has been some overlap between these stages, but each have unique characteristics that define the era and the people working within it. Technology innovations have disrupted previous paradigms, and leadership mechanisms should have seen similar disruption too. However, it seems that even as we reinvent the world on the back of our tremendous innovations, we continue to rely on tried-and-true (read: 'archaic') methods of maximizing our production.

Where has this lack of progression in the science and practice of leadership led us, but to a world where only 15% of employed people report being engaged at work! There is a strong correlation between employee engagement and employee productivity: Disengaged employees equal reduced production.[1] Reduced production leads to reduced spending, and/or the rapid accumulation of debt. Debt can lead to lower consumer confidence and the slowing of other key economic indicators—which is why this subject should be at the top of the board's agenda at every Fortune 500 company.

Resistance to change

Why is low employee engagement not resulting in a revolution in management practice? Perhaps for the same reason that we have had alternative methods of clean energy production for decades and alarming evidence that we are in the midst of a climate crisis, yet we are still burning more fossil fuels than ever. Change is hard. Rather than appealing to our better natures and promoting our need to strive for self-actualization, businesses appeal to our baser natures by stimulating us to chase what is obtained with relative ease: Food, clothing, shelter, status, and creature comforts. This is what equates to wealth in our current society, not greater safety, more love, better esteem, or higher social impact.

A new revolution in leadership

Now we understand some of the reasons why the practice of human motivation (aka leadership) has lagged, despite the damaging effects of attempting to fit square-peg leadership into a round hole society. C-suites and boardrooms are highly reluctant to introduce the kind of radical change needed to solve the global engagement crisis. That is why this manifesto is not addressed to them (I'll leave that to Gallup).[2]

If you are still reading this, it's likely because you believe (as I do) that the wave of change to upend the leadership status quo will not be a movement catalyzed in the halls of power. This revolution will be spearheaded by new managers, frontliners, and those described as middle management.

I'm appealing to those of you in this segment of the leadership population because you have suffered long enough.

You've committed to enterprises whose so-called noble missions are paper-thin.

You've been left holding the bag when restructures have been required because of sales targets you had nothing to do with.

Your guidance has been ignored time and again when it comes to what adds value to customers and the people you aim to serve.

You've been given a boatload of stress, but no capability to lead at the most crucial level of any company: Supporting those who interact with the customer.

You've been given some training, sure, like courses with nice names such as 'situational coaching' and 'high-performance management.' Still, you find it a struggle to align the needs of developing your people versus delivering results.

Because you are measured on bringing in the numbers, nine times out of ten your development—and that of your team—falls by the wayside.

Well, all of that stops now.

Together, we are going to go on a journey informed by management science, from luminaries such as Abraham H. Maslow, Stephen R. Covey, Patrick Lencioni, Jim Collins, Tom Rath, Donald O. Clifton, John C. Maxwell, James C. Hunter, and Simon Sinek, to name but a few. Forgive the lack of diversity in this group. These thought leaders each have important contributions in describing the need for a leadership revolution.

I'm calling this latest epoch Leadership 3.0—or the Age of Servant Leadership.

Let's look at how we arrived at this crucial juncture.

Leadership 1.0: Command and control

Leadership 1.0 was the period from the end of the American Civil War through the beginning of the American Industrial Revolution, up until the end of World War II. This era was characterized by poorly educated, low-skill rural workers migrating from farms into cities in search of valuable manufacturing jobs. The assembly-line approach to productivity was invented to motivate performance, and line management was born as an offshoot of the overseer role dominating the agricultural age. Most men had some degree of military background due to national and global conflict, and top-down hierarchy was deemed the most efficient way for private-sector organizations to operate.

The immigration boom came during the same period, as people the world over left their shores for America in search of streets paved with gold and a land of milk and honey. Still, despite classist barriers, hard work and self-determinism became the hallmarks of the greatest leaders of the age: Rockefeller in oil, Carnegie in steel, and Ford in transportation.[3] (In my estimation, Henry Ford and his Model T automobile defined this process-powered era with the adoption of the assembly-line—originally used in slaughterhouses—which transformed how commodities were produced.) These industries were top-down-led, mass-production-focused, customization-averse, and hard-work-powered, and following the chain of command was rewarded.

In short, *Leadership 1.0* was about individual determinism: Your lifestyle was proportionate to your level of opportunity, how hard you worked, and how well you either commanded or followed commands.

Leadership 2.0: Societal change

World War I and II dramatically shifted the corporate status quo, as women began holding down some jobs previously unavailable to them. With the men away fighting, American women began to develop new capabilities and a desire for greater independence.[4] The civil rights movement of the 1960s further diversified the workforce, as disenfranchised African Americans began to climb the social, economic, and class ladders. And in the backdrop of all this societal change, new technologies—principally, the first computers—began to shift the economy from a purely manufacturing base to new services and opportunities.

This is *Leadership 2.0*, where hierarchy still reigned supreme but had to be applied to types of people far less inculcated in military ways of working. As immigrants, women, and African Americans began to reshape the corporate landscape, teamwork and managing diversity to achieve goals became crucial.

The archetype of this phase is President John F. Kennedy and his space race. To bind diverse groups of people together, leaders needed to both inspire and manage performance standards for the first time. Individual determinism was assisted by team and technology.

Lest we forget, it took a team of African American women to solve the key problems and equations of launching a rocket into space.[5] Leadership was still largely in step with the needs of society and its constituents, but that would not last for long.

Between the late 1970s and the mid-2000s, the American middle class expanded and largely prospered.[6] New conveniences were around every corner as technology moved to the forefront of business and society. New and previously unheard-of industries emerged, as industrialization gave rise to the modern service economy. Although many of these companies sought to disrupt the status quo, ultimately they were corrupted by short-term gain and profit for a few at the expense of the labor of many.

This workforce was the most diverse in history, not only in terms of ethnicity, sex, and nationality, but also in terms of sexual orientation, gender, and generational mix.[7] Leaders dabbled in a few new techniques to generate value and productivity, but largely maintained the status quo established in *Leadership 2.0*. It was during this period that thinking global but acting local, 'vitality curves,' matrix organizations, and open offices were born. Corporations added better, more inclusive words to their mission statements and made some moderate progress to become more socially responsible, even as individual dynamism continued to be disproportionately rewarded. Take for example, Johnson & Johnson (the personal care company), with its modern diversity and inclusion mission:

"For all employees to draw on their unique experiences and backgrounds together—to spark solutions that create a better, healthier world."

Workers, clamoring for a seat at the table, began to disrupt the status quo by voting with their feet. Employee retention, brain drain, and talent wars characterized the era, along with a precipitous drop in employee engagement and productivity. The number of disenfranchised people rose, and leadership had few good answers. Meanwhile, companies reorganized into work groups, hierarchies flattened, the agile method was born, and responsibility became more specialized. Leveraging technology became standard operating procedure, as organizations sought out the best way to harness digital, data, and analytics to improve performance. Women, ethnic minorities, and millennial's occupied more seats of authority than ever before—but still not enough to upset the defined order of *Leadership 2.0*.

Leadership 3.0: A new era

It is within this context that we currently find ourselves. Individual dynamism leads to far less productivity than group exceptionalism assisted by technology. Unfortunately, most leaders of the *Leadership 2.0* period are at a loss for how to respond to the desires of people with drastically different lifestyles, talents, needs, motivations, and preferred recognition types than themselves.

The one-size-fits-all approach of *Leadership 2.0* must be replaced by an intense focus on the intrinsic capabilities of each individual, and the potential synergies within each group of people.

Trust is the currency of *Leadership 3.0*, because we are living through arguably one of the most tumultuous ages in history.

Leaders capable of inspiring, engaging, aligning, coaching, and coaxing out individual and team brilliance are more in need than ever before.

Hence the reason for this manifesto. These pages provide a blueprint for how to lead in this age of technology and group exceptionalism.

Paradoxically, the answer does not lie in systems but in humanity.

The more technology pervades our lives, the greater our need for clarity, courage, caring, culture, and talent cultivation—all things that machines cannot create for us.

We cannot wait for C-suite executives to respond appropriately to this crisis.

We—the managers responsible for the people who create value for our companies—must do this for ourselves, and our people.

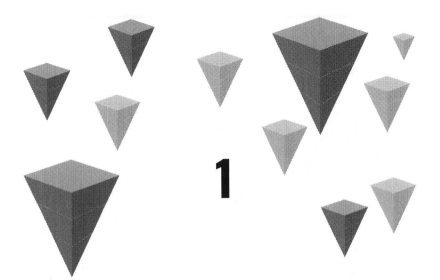

What Is Servant Leadership?

The top-down hierarchical model of organizational design and leadership has been the dominant form for decades. Although this model has remained stubbornly entrenched for the reasons outlined previously in the Introduction, other approaches to organizational design have been adopted by some successful companies and introduced by leadership experts such as:

- Donald O. Clifton, who introduced 'positive psychology' into the management lexicon[8]

- Patrick Lencioni, who demonstrated the importance of trust for team performance[9]

- John C. Maxwell, who wrote the blueprints for modern team leadership[10]

- Jim Collins, who disrupted the leadership status quo with well-researched insights[11]

- Simon Sinek, who showcased the importance of placing mission and organization purpose ahead of profit[12]

Reinventing the leadership hierarchy

You also might be familiar with the concept of the inverted hierarchy of leadership, first introduced by Robert Greenleaf:[13] Rather than an organization oriented to a small group of influencers, instead, the organization orients itself to support the value creators within it who typically act in service of the customer (Figure 1). Organizations that dedicate themselves to encouraging those who support the customer need not only to invert the hierarchy, but also to reinvent the job descriptions of its leaders at all levels. Thus emerges the need for servant leaders.

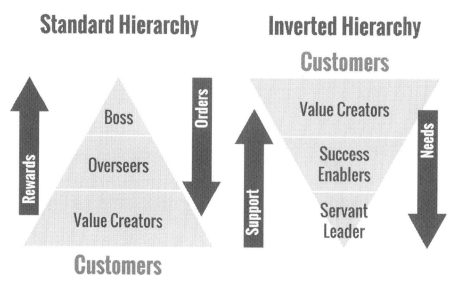

Figure 1: Standard organizational hierarchy versus inverted hierarchy

Serving those who create value for the customer can manifest in a variety of ways, but it all starts with being highly in tune with the customer's needs and the barriers that your team faces in overdelivering on those needs. As these needs and barriers are identified, the servant leader-run team commits to, and prioritizes, solving these issues as an organizational imperative. There is a constant free-flow of communication from the value creators to the problem solvers, then back from the problem solvers to the value creators.

Many teams organized in this manner regularly report higher trust scores, engagement, and productivity because they feel well supported by their leadership, know that their leaders are in tune with their challenges, and understand that their leaders are always actively working to resolve them.

How does organizational hierarchy affect teams?

Gallup's Q12 assessment on employee engagement demonstrates the importance of these attributes for teams, with the following questions: [14]

1. Do you know what is expected of you at work?

2. Do you have the materials and equipment to do your work right?

3. At work, do you have the opportunity to do what you do best every day?

4. In the last seven days, have you received recognition or praise for doing good work?

5. Does your supervisor, or someone at work, seem to care about you as a person?

6. Is there someone at work who encourages your development?

7. At work, do your opinions seem to count?

8. Does the mission/purpose of your company make you feel your job is important?

9. Are your associates (fellow employees) committed to doing quality work?

10. Do you have a best friend at work?

11. In the last six months, has someone at work talked to you about your progress?

12. In the last year, have you had opportunities to learn and grow?

Because the 'serve' in servant leadership really relates to understanding, identification of needs, analysis, problem-solving, communication, and agility, this may not be such a leap for today's leaders. The big difference is the overarching culture created by servant leaders: Over time, the people being led in this fashion really begin to trust and believe that their voice is highly valued, but then a flood of problems comes into the organization.

Don't fret, this is the sign that the culture is working! The true benefit of this approach is the quick transition from customer need to response and solution. Moreover, customer engagement and retention are transformed, because customers *know* that their feedback matters, and that they have a willing partner who regularly goes above and beyond to bring them value-added solutions.

Leadership styles and their impact on teams

You might have heard of the four stages of group formation, defined by Bruce Tuckman in 1965[15]:

1. Forming

2. Storming

3. Norming

4. Performing

These are still scientifically valid today. In stage 1, teams form around a new leader, teammates, or mission. In stages 2 and 3, they routinely disagree about how to accomplish the goal, and 'storm' until effective norms are established. In stage 4, once trust, commitment, accountability, and results focus are increased, the team can perform the task at hand effectively.

When faced with forming a team, the top-down leader dominates with one version of the truth: theirs, or their boss's. They don't engage with the whole team and are only concerned with the end result— so the kind of norms that establish usually relate to satisfying the leader, whether or not they facilitate group cohesion. In these teams, performance can only be as good as the talent and resilience to manage their difficult bosses' expectations. When results are achieved, the leader absorbs the lion's share of the credit, and when things go wrong, the leader distributes blame to their team rather than accept ultimate accountability. These leaders are likely to be out of touch with both their customer-facing team's complaints and their customers' needs. Because they spend so much time managing up and playing politics, they achieve few truly impactful results.

In contrast, servant leaders can create high-performing teams faster than top-down leaders, because this approach effectively hacks many of the stages of group development.

Because servant leaders are intent listeners rather than dictators, they:

- Gather the risks, fears, anxieties, and worries of the team related to the task

- Dedicate themselves to clarifying, coaching, and coaxing solutions out of each team member

- Master getting teams to self-organize around agreed ways of working to resolve disputes, make decisions, reward progress, and mitigate risk

- Focus their team's attention on increasing the speed and efficiency of response to customer needs and overcoming inevitable barriers on the path to achievement.

Implementing the principles of servant leadership

This raises an important question. If you work within a top-down organizational culture, can you still implement servant leadership principles? Well, organizational culture is not actually a static thing.[16] It ebbs and flows, depending on the style and preferences of senior leadership.

I have actually never worked for a company that is fully oriented toward the people who create value for the customer; however, I have always oriented my individual teams or enterprises in this way-effectively establishing my own culture within the overall company culture.

Remember: To your people, you are the company-and it is not only your right, but your imperative, to define how your team operates.

Now that you know what servant leadership is, how can you progress from where you are today and begin implementing these principles? In the coming pages you will see:

- How servant leadership starts from within

- How servant leadership requires a radical shift in attitude related to the leader's role

- How to wield the power of positive psychology

- Why team talent outweighs individual talent every time, and how to unlock it

- How to reframe the 'game' of business for your team and organization

- What love has to do with leadership

Once you finish this part of your journey, you will receive a bevy of inspiration from the best minds in leadership to increase your leadership impact, beginning today.

Let's get started!

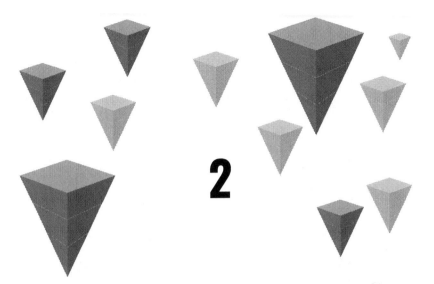

How to Manifest Personal Effectiveness

No leader is perfect. What we deem perfection is often just the manifestation of a powerful combination of desirable traits related to personal effectiveness. I call this M.H.T.:

Mindset
Habits
Tracking

Some leaders' mindsets, habits, and commitment levels just happen to be so potent that it makes us mere mortals feel as if we can never aspire to their levels of excellence and achievement. This chapter will endeavor to show you that anyone with the right M.H.T. can boost their own personal effectiveness and, in turn, their capabilities as a servant leader.

Identifying leadership strengths

One exercise I like to do with groups is to ask them to identify the top strengths of their favorite leaders. More often than not, participants name individuals such as Dr. Martin Luther King, Greta Thunberg, Steve Jobs, Michelle Obama, Abraham Lincoln, Oprah Winfrey,

Muhammad Ali, Jack Ma, and Walt Disney. What is interesting and revealing about this activity is that while each of these individuals have undoubtedly left their mark on society at large, the way they have gone about it is distinctly their own—which is the point. There is no intrinsic magic formula or recipe for great accomplishment, no such thing as pre-destiny. These are normal people, possessed of a different outlook on life, habits that reinforced their strengths, and a strong sense of responsibility and accountability.

Take Dr. Martin Luther King, for example.

As a person of deep faith and conviction, Dr. King inspired millions to protest racial inequality in America. He had a gift and flair for oratory with little rival in modern history.

One little-recognized strength was his strategic capability, which allowed him to outmaneuver President Lyndon B. Johnson at his own game of politics. He also had deep reservoirs of steely resolve that never bent or broke, despite innumerable death threats, blackmail, and inhumane treatment in the various prisons where he was detained for exercising his right to free speech.

He never allowed his mind to entertain failure. He honed his gift for public speaking in the pulpits of the South and ensured that forward progress was always achieved.

Let's turn to a contrasting example, that of Steve Jobs: A genius who helped shape the modern age.

Deeply idiosyncratic, Steve Jobs possessed a mastery of influence so powerful that he could convince himself and others to distort reality. But his true greatness was in his obsessive attention to detail and ability to visualize, communicate, and manifest his version of the future.

However, it must also be said that he was not the best person to work with. He berated employees, denied his co-founders their well-earned stock in Apple, and disavowed his first daughter Lisa's parentage.[17]

To be clear, I am not upholding Steve Jobs as an example of servant leadership; rather, I am illustrating how his mindset of perfection or nothing, his habit of tirelessly searching for and developing innovation, and his ability to make progress at an outstanding clip allowed him to produce an astounding legacy in only fifty-six years.

Defining successful leadership

Can you see the ties that bind a peace-touting activist and a futurist inventor? While these leaders had different M.H.T.s, they shared one important attribute:

> **Early on they defined a purpose for their lives: A mission that they were willing to invest everything they possessed to realize.**

For without a purpose beyond accumulating wealth, the need for M.H.T. greatly diminishes. Whether we are speaking of Walt Disney, who invested all of his resources in creating Disneyland when everyone thought he was crazy, or Muhammad Ali, who lost his championship title at the height of his career and millions in potential earnings to protest the Vietnam War, what differentiates legendary leaders from the rest of us are the deeply held beliefs that drive their mindset, habits, and degree of personal commitment.

Employees today are disengaged largely because they are seeking purpose and finding falsehood.

> **One of the defining traits of a servant leader at any organizational level is a clearly defined motive behind the work to which they commit themselves and their teams.**

The difference is how a servant leader goes about motivating his or her people to achieve.

In *Good to Great,* Jim Collins and his team of researchers showed that the most successful companies were led by what they called 'Level 5 leaders.'[18] They defined Level 5 leadership as a paradoxical combination of humility and intense personal will. This gives us a clue as to what these leaders tweaked in their approach or naturally possessed, which enabled spectacular and sustainable financial performance.

Can humility and will be developed? Of course they can!

- What makes a person humble?
- Is it one's upbringing, values, or environment?

27

- Is it a personality trait that only a few people possess?

- Are these leaders somehow otherwise enlightened?

Let's look at the M.H.T. factors to find out.

Mindset

It's true that humble people certainly seem to be more curious about the world around them than egocentric folks who believe the world revolves around them. This curiosity sparks questioning, searching, studying, and analyzing everything relevant—not to find any particular answers, but as an exercise in reminding them that the more they learn, the more they realize they don't know.

It is this rejection of 'knowing it all' that defines how they lead. Because they are wise enough to know they are not the font of all truth, they inspire brilliance from those around them. Humility leads to questioning, which drives understanding and, in turn, derives solutions.

Servant leaders focus on learning, diagnosing, and analyzing, rather than blaming, shaming, and denigrating employees for not having all the answers at their fingertips.

Humility requires leaders to be the first to admit that they don't know it all—not as an excuse, but as a call to action to constantly explore and deepen understanding.

What defines the mindset of the humble leader? First, humility should never be confused with passivity or conflict avoidance. Humility is the mindset that recognizes brutal facts before deciding how to act. (This is why I don't admire Steve Jobs, despite all his accomplishments. According to Walter Isaacson's deep biography,[19] Jobs regularly distorted facts to suit his liking and schedule, and in so doing, forced others into alignment or direct conflict with him.) And because leadership is not a zero-sum game, one's achievements are only as worthy as the journey to achieve them.

Humble people recognize that there are few things over which we have complete control, and in order to be an effective leader, Stephen R.

Covey writes that one must 'be proactive'[20] in order to distinguish clearly between what is worrisome or concerning and what is truly actionable.

One additional mindset that humility brings to the table is awareness that the leader is only as good as the team around them. Humble leaders are neither autocratic nor laissez-faire. They leverage their team's collective wisdom and the power of productive conflict to sharpen decision-making. Then, they leverage shared accountability to tackle the tasks before them.

A servant leader needs to embody humility, which means brutal facts are respected, proactivity is required, and the team is the cornerstone of effective decision-making.

Habits

Will is developed by discipline, consistency, and commitment. Think of it as a reservoir that requires a regular, steady influx of rainwater to fill. It is all about testing one's resolve, or answering the question, 'How badly do I want this?'—which brings us back to purpose.

There is also an important element of wish fulfillment. It feels good to stay the course--to wake up at 5am each day, training for that marathon you ultimately complete. Will knows that the future is created by the habits of today—both positive and negative.

As we've seen, humility is the mindset of a servant leader, while will is the commitment to positive habits that reinforce that mindset, building the resolve and knowledge that most goals can be achieved with the right routines in place. Will is constructed over time—day after day—until it becomes an automatic, inspiring attribute. When people see a leader's consistency of behavior and quality of decision-making, despite all the chaos happening around them, they feel more confident and trust that the whole team will come out the other side intact!

Another key differentiator between Collins's Level 5 leadership and servant leadership is the concept of caring. Servant leaders put care into every aspect of their job, but it's most evident in the form of commitment to supporting their teams through thick and thin. This care makes them want to:

- Know each team member at a fundamental human level

- Get to know their individual aspirations and goals

- Build plans together, leading to the achievement of individual goals (which links back to team goals)

Tracking

Just as a great personal trainer cares deeply about, takes a heightened interest in, and actively supports building the commitment of each client, so does a servant leader transform commitment into something tangible that can be visualized, tracked, and measured. By offering this enhanced degree of support to help teammates understand their potential and commit to the necessary deliverables to get there, the servant leader transforms their care into confidence and, ultimately, conquests.

Servant leaders understand that personal effectiveness creates the reservoir of will needed to lead with positivity, proactivity, and passion.

If the leader is stressed out, out of shape, anxious, depressed, unstable, lethargic, checked out, or overly negative, then this will permeate the entire organization.

Personalizing M.H.T. is a four-step process:

1. Define your own purpose and energizing mission (reading *Find Your Why* by Simon Sinek is a great place to start[21])

2. Translate that mission into short-, medium-, and long-term goals

3. Convert those goals into the daily activities (habits) needed to manifest these objectives into reality

4. Demonstrate commitment to your mission and purpose by diligently tracking progress and achievements and making the necessary course corrections along the way

The way you lead yourself is the same way you lead your teams.

The greatest leaders in history led themselves in such a way that they inspired intense followership. Servant leaders don't ask teammates to do anything that they would be unwilling to do themselves. M.H.T. is the formula for ensuring that this is a fact, not just lip service.

The benefits of increasing personal effectiveness for leaders are clear.

You will gain more energy, enthusiasm, positivity, proactivity, intensity, and resilience to take on greater challenges and reap the rewards of doing so.

You will become a role model of walking the talk. The self-discipline to maintain a proactive mindset, focus on the right habits, and hold yourself accountable to your commitments daily is contagious.

This is what separates servant leaders from the rest of the pack.

Luck never enters the equation.

When you learn to combine your natural leadership talents with the M.H.T. approach to personal effectiveness, you are well on your way to becoming a true servant leader.

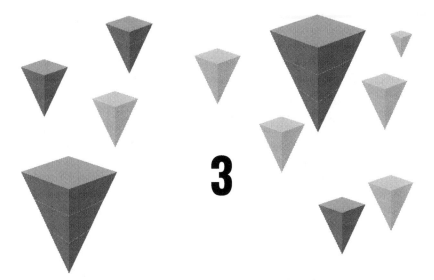

Use Influence, Not Authority

Today, the jobs of line managers are tougher than ever before. With the stress of perpetually performing and little tolerance for setbacks, and the expectation that one should be a values role model and expert people developer, the job seems built to make sustainable success against all these axes impossible to achieve. This is why, when faced with these contradictory imperatives, many managers prioritize almost to a fault the financial result, and to a lesser degree required compliance with the desired standards. Personal development usually becomes something done infrequently, due to the more pressing and more valued aspects of the managerial job description.

What do managers receive in return for all this stress, that makes the pains of the job worthwhile? Certainly, there are improved financial rewards, versus what individual contributors receive. And for many managers, the other reward is far more insidious: Having the power to control others' lives. The ego boost that comes with knowing that people have to do your bidding is a huge motivator for many people seeking managerial roles.

Managers embody the organization

This is where slippery-slope to rock-bottom employee engagement really accelerates. Never forget: To employees, the manager *is* the company. Its culture, mission, values, policies, priorities, strategies, and programs are *all* filtered through managers. When managers are more concerned with managing their higher-ups' perception of them than supporting the people who generate value for the company, those people quickly check out, head to greener pastures, or, worse still, replace the manager when they move up or out of the organization.

The only thing worse than a power-hungry manager is the person who is promoted to follow them—the apple doesn't fall far from the tree.

Still, you do have a choice in how you choose to behave as a manager and team leader. Just because your higher-ups are short-term-oriented and egocentric does not mean you have to pay that forward to your own people. A great manager can operate as an umbrella, sheltering the team from negative influences coming down from above. By doing so, the filter through which employees experience the company culture is dramatically different.

How to influence others, with the right kind of authority

The case for seeking influence over authority is simple. Influence is the art of persuading others to adopt a cause as their own, and because of this sense of ownership, to do whatever is necessary to achieve the goal.

Influence does not require a title, role, higher salary, or status. Its primary aim is to achieve agreement, alignment, and action.

It is a more pervasive, subtle, elegant, and ultimately sustainable method of getting things done.

Authority exists to increase its own sense of worth. Authority is rife with insecurity, because it knows that no one takes it seriously without acquired status. Authority always has to respond to a higher authority, which limits its flexibility, creativity, and autonomy to execute initiatives. Even though it acts extremely confident, authority needs constant reassurance and validation that its ideas really are the best way to do things.

Servant leaders never need to seek authority, because they understand that the mission is bigger than themselves.

Because of this belief, they dedicate themselves to focusing on what they can control and augmenting their sphere of influence—not to gain status, but to serve the needs of their teams better. Servant leaders want a seat at the decision-making table. They work to become masters of influencing without authority in all directions—with their peers, higher-ups, and across functions. They wield influence to keep the needs of the customer, and the people they support, at the forefront of every key decision.

Authority wielders—or bosses—are the dumpers of the business world. As mentioned in Chapter 1, when directives are issued from their bosses, managers simply pass it all down to their unwitting subordinates, rather than filtering, pushing back, or prioritizing. Then they ride their people until they can claim to their bosses how they individually triumphed at those tasks.

They are the embodiment of status-quo guardians who abhor change, resisting any attempt to distribute power more evenly throughout the organization.

Trust is key

How, then, is influence gained in an organization, if not through positional power? The answer, in a word, is *trust*.

The reason why servant leaders can coexist successfully—and even outcompete their more egocentric, bossy counterparts—is because higher-ups are confident in their ability to deliver. In truth, executive leadership cares less about how performance is achieved (as long as it complies with rules and regulations) than what is achieved. If you can achieve consistent results without burning people out or throwing them under a bus, you will gain just as much (or even more) trust and respect within your organization as someone who commands and controls their way to results.

When criteria other than numbers are applied to managers, those who drive performance and cultivate an environment of high engagement rise to the top of the crop in nearly every company.

Bosses can create environments where unreasonable demands for skewed standards of perfection and complete fealty destroy any chance for team cohesion.

In contrast, servant leaders break through superficial invulnerability to expose the humanity beneath. Their teams know their performance expectations, but also that they are not alone in pursuing results. Their manager is right there at every step, to support their progress and stimulate their brilliance. Weakness is not only tolerated—it is exposed, regularly discussed during feedback sessions, and often mitigated by the others' strengths in the group, if not by the manager themselves. Team talents are reinforced, combined, and leveraged to achieve success with far less stress and effort than the top-down approach.

How to acquire trust and build influence

While there is no hard-and-fast formula for trust-building, the 'people-first' orientation of servant leaders is a great starting place. When you show honest interest in a person beyond the role they serve in the organization, you gain their respect. This evolves as your team perceives the degree to which you are open and vulnerable about your own shortcomings, weaknesses, and even lessons from past failures: This communicates to them that perfection is not the standard, but learning and improving as a result of failure is required.

Trust takes another leap forward when you are perceived as someone who is clear about expectations, does not play favorites, and meets each person where they are on their journey to deliver—not only directing as necessary, but coaching, inspiring, and empowering them as appropriate. Finally, when people know you are transparent and honest in all your dealings with them, their last barriers to believing, trusting, and following your lead usually fall away.

Increased influence is the direct result of trust-building: It works with peers, higher-ups, and across functions as well as with subordinates, but the tactics are slightly different in each instance. What builds trust with each person is highly individualized and specific. Having a frank discussion about trust-builders and trust-breakers with these key collaborators is an important step to becoming ultimately more influential in your collective dealings.

Make notes of what builds and breaks trust with each person and establish a simple contract that if you step over the trust-breaker line in any instance, your colleague will immediately provide you feedback—and you offer to do the same in return. Then, regularly revisit this process over time to ensure that your relationship is deepening and becoming more immune to the inevitable disappointments and disagreements that occur in the day-to-day.

Don't be a boss, be a Jedi

Leveraging positional authority may be a faster and more direct way to achievement, but it leads to a series of negative habits that not only become difficult to break, but ultimately limit your career potential in today's evolving workplace. Directing is the weakest form of influence: People usually only adhere because they must, to keep their jobs. Obsessing about eradicating weakness in people—or, even worse, trying to develop it into strength—leads to a dramatic dispersion of resources that would be better suited to being leveraged to enhance the existing strengths of the organization's human capital. Moreover, maintaining alignment and agreement is nearly impossible when you are disliked and not respected. And focusing on reinforcing and entrenching one's positional authority instead of developing one's capabilities and continuously stretching and improving means eventually being passed by when someone more agile, positive, and influential shows up.

Bosses are becoming extinct, mainly because companies can no longer afford the cost of such people on the organization's culture. In some instances and specific industries, these individuals are still being rewarded disproportionately for the *blitzkrieg* approach to management; but thankfully, this is an area where leadership experts have made the most headway with senior management in changing the status quo. Increasingly, metrics beyond the bottom line are being employed to measure managerial performance, including engagement surveys, 360-degree evaluations, where you receive feedback from higher-ups, peers, and subordinates, and integrity hotlines, which allow for anonymous feedback on bad behavior. If you're still pursuing the boss path in 2020, this is why you may find yourself on a pretty short runway.

Servant leaders wield influence like Jedi wield the Force. They are able to tap into it at will and manifest its power, continuously improving the environment for their people to perform. They are masters of knowing when to be diplomatic, and when to advocate their position. They are unafraid to challenge conventional wisdom, if conventional wisdom is not making things better for the customer. And usually, their disciples permeate throughout the organization much faster than followers of the boss model. They become the pillars of employee engagement and productivity and are more involved in high-level decision-making than others.

One personal example is back when I was a veritable peon working out of Turkey for a global pharmaceuticals company, where I was responsible for a mature portfolio of products.

I saw a need to accelerate the region's digital journey and influenced my boss to let me add this responsibility to my job description. Then, I influenced a senior leader by telling her that we could not wait for this change to happen and ended up leading a global project to evaluate the customer relationship management platform that would be at the heart of the digital ecosystem we were seeking to manifest.

As the project progressed and the cost of acquiring such a new capability ballooned to more than $30 million, the CEO balked and put his foot down- publicly stating that such a project would not be funded, as it was not an organizational priority.

Knowing the pain that the sales reps were experiencing with the existing platform and feeling passionate about how we could transform the customer experience on the back of this platform, I convinced my senior sponsor to simply ask for a 90-minute meeting to thoroughly explain our proposal.

In the intervening days between his agreement and the meeting, I sent out a survey to every general manager in the world, enlisting their feedback to create the burning platform for change. The response was so overwhelmingly in favor of the change that when the international head of the pharmaceuticals business read the proposal, he cancelled the meeting and approved the project immediately-no discussion necessary.

As a project leader I had no real authority. But I had the courage of my convictions, passion, coalition-building ability, advocacy, and inquiry skills that I expertly leveraged to achieve our end goal, despite having only joined the company 18 months prior.

If I had waited until I had enough authority to simply pull out the checkbook, that change never would have happened. It was only my orientation toward the customer and customer-serving teams that allowed me to effectively influence this outcome.

Because servant leaders are people developers by nature, and are obsessed with creating value for the customer, they leave large legacies and are much harder to replace than less-capable managers.

Servant leaders' value is known in the market. Even more telling, whenever they leave a company, the people whom they have previously led are usually happy and compelled to join them. As such, their influence never really diminishes—it just shifts from one employer to the next, for the benefit of the latter and the detriment of the former.

Be assertive, not aggressive

Let's return, then, to the conundrum for today's managers.

Rather than simply succumbing to the pressure of delivering short-term results, push back if you are not involved in target-setting, or disagree with the targets being requested.

Question any decision or policy that does not improve conditions for your team or makes serving the customer more difficult (unless it relates to breach of conduct).

Ensure you are fairly measured across the full spectrum of your responsibilities.

Commit to people support and development as the primary mechanism to achieve your objectives.

Demand further development of skills and capabilities that augment your influence and future opportunities within the organization.

Remember: Without your alignment, agreement, and action, the company will grind to a standstill.

Sitting there, reading this wherever you may be, you already possess tremendous influence over the direction of your company—should you choose to apply it. The company's value creators always possess more power than the few leaders at the top: It's time that those in positional power are reminded that we will no longer stand for this unlevel playing field, where loyalty is rewarded over honesty, and where true leaders are sidelined in favor of people playing politics and managing perception.

Let's use this influence to abolish positional authority—especially if it doesn't add value to our people, our lives, or our missions!

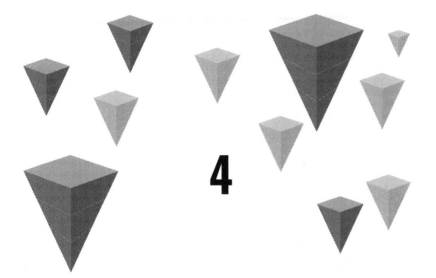

How to Leverage Positive Psychology for Success

Have you ever had a leader who focused almost exclusively on what was right or special about you, rather than what was wrong with you? Unfortunately, most people have never experienced this leadership phenomenon. Those who have count these people as lifelong coaches and mentors and usually progress quite quickly as a result. The rest of us have had to deal with an unending litany of people obsessed with curing us of our weaknesses.

From public speaking classes to performance development and feedback on organizing our email inboxes more efficiently, this focus on weakness and self-improvement is another reason employee disengagement is rampant. Who wants to work for someone who fails to value you beyond your task performance? But most of us go on with the program and dutifully place weakness-fixing tasks into our personal development plans for the following year—and at the end of that year, most of us keep receiving the same messages about our lack of development.

When this approach is applied on an enterprise scale, the negative implications for motivation are dramatic. Which raises the question: 'Why doesn't eliminating weaknesses lead to breakout performance?'

How do we define weakness?

First, we need to understand what 'weakness' is, because depending on our definition, our mindset toward the issue shifts. Is weakness defined as an absence of strength, as with a scrawny teenager trying to bench-press 135 pounds for the first time? Or is it the downside of an existing talent, like a perfectionist who is considered overly demanding on himself and others? Maybe it's both. Lack of capability combined with lack of awareness would make for a more complete definition of weakness. Certainly, the kid can become much stronger if he dedicates himself to regular weight training, but if his obsession with perfection isolates him from others, would we truly consider him strong?

It all depends on what is being valued. If our young man in this example is training to be a professional bodybuilder, all that matters is his ability to accumulate physical mass and definition. If his trainers are weakness-oriented, they will focus on why he is not training hard enough, eating correctly, or concentrating on improving. However, eventually, we will learn if the young man has the genetic and obsessive capability to stand out among all other young men in the same pursuit of physical perfection. And there will be physical limits he cannot push past without risking serious injury. Is the person who comes in fifth place in a bodybuilding contest considered weak?

However, say he is not an athlete but a leader in student government. His penchant for perfectionism is likely to alienate him from his supporters despite his intellect, charisma, and take-charge attitude. What is most valued is his ability to win debates, regardless of tactics. If his academic advisers are weakness-focused, they are likely to encourage him to improve his diplomacy. He'll certainly learn some new approaches to dealing with people in a better way, but the likelihood that diplomacy will become his defining trait years later as a U.S. senator is extremely low.

Change your view of weakness

Gallup, the organization behind the popular Clifton Strengths Assessment, defines a strength as a natural way of thinking, behaving, or doing that can be productively applied. [22] Weakness is when this same natural way of thinking, behaving, or doing is either not productively applied, or worse, destructively applied.

When you take the Clifton Strengths Top 34 Assessment, you receive a report of your top talents in order of descending dominance (where 1 = most dominant, and 34 = least dominant).

Gallup-certified strengths coaches are quick to point out that talent 34 is not actually a weakness; it is just a person's least dominant, present or active talent. The idea is that the absence of a talent is only a weakness the moment you try to apply it.

For example, if I were to attempt to kick a football 50 yards and fall short of the mark, it doesn't really mean I'm a weak kicker. It means that I have never had to apply this capability.

If, as Gallup states, weakness is an inherent part of strength, what happens when you focus on developing it? The better question is: how do you go about *developing* the flipside of something that actually is a talent when productively applied? We'll discuss this in greater detail later in this chapter, but for now just let the question percolate in your mind.

There is a telling study from the 1950s, about how reading speed could be increased by a variety of different teaching methods.[23]

The study, of approximately 6,000 tenth graders, found that the methods had less impact on reading speed than who actually did the teaching. What was even more surprising than the lack of methodological impact was the finding that students who already read more than 300 words per minute at the outset of the study improved their speed nearly 10 times to 2,900 words per minute post-development intervention!

They became even better at what they were already good at, whereas the slower reading group did not even come close. The implications of this are extraordinary: There may be no ceiling to how good you can be in the areas where you have natural proclivity.

We see this most often in child prodigies or exceptional athletes. With proper training and coaching, these individuals can become truly best in class with their given set of talents. Everyone else can become better, but not in the same league. It's a question of focus, orientation, and prioritization.

Catching people doing things right, and putting these folks in their strength zone, is a more effective way to deliver results than harping on underdeveloped capabilities and skills.

Expand your concept of performance

However, the brutal truth of business is that our definition of performance is too narrow to catch people being brilliant. We want them to excel in the ways that matter most to our organization, whether or not that is actually their area of greatest capability.

For example, I am an award-winning, bestselling fiction novelist who also works at a pharmaceutical company. No one has explored how my obvious writing talents could be best exploited for the benefits of my enterprise.

Similarly, the finance professional who is a brilliant social networker or the marketer who is a natural communicator when placed in front of teams may be undervalued for these skills. We value the finance professional most for his or her ability to manage profit and loss and maintain appropriate financial controls, and we value the marketer for his or her ability to create strategic plans that are successfully implemented on time and on budget.

Of course, this is not to say that companies are not valuing the right things; rather, they continuously miss opportunities to capitalize on everything their employees can bring to the table. It's really counterintuitive when you think about it. Everyone complains about capacity and efficiency, and most enterprises are leveraging less than 50% of the people potential in their midst.

Human resources (HR) is valued not for extracting this potential, but for managing the cost base of the organization while overseeing large-scale programs such as performance management and

44

development. Employee engagement is tracked and measured by HR, but usually with scant consequences for leaders who deliver financial performance while creating low engagement cultures.

If it isn't HR's job to maximize the human potential within organizations, guess whose responsibility it is?

Managers, of course—most of whom are ill-equipped to assess and build talent and capabilities. Managers are inundated with performance directives from their bosses, administrative burden, and people problems.

Shift your mindset

What's a manager to do, if they want to unlock the hidden potential of their team? First, they need to shift their mindset in terms of what they value most and shift psychologically to extract the most value from their people.

The mindset shift is away *from* the way that performance is currently being managed internally, and *toward* how the customer values company performance. And the psychological shift is *from* focusing on developing weakness *to* identifying talents and developing them into strengths, while mitigating any behavioral or competency derailers.

Let's take two sales professionals as an example.

Ted is tremendous at overdelivering against the numbers. He is highly technical and persuasive: Even when the customer doesn't necessarily want to buy, he finds himself somehow coerced into doing so. Ted is arrogant and boastful within the team about his accomplishments, and because his territory represents 25% of the district's total, he is regularly recognized and rewarded as one of the top salespeople in the company. Ted's manager largely ignores his impact on others, telling new team members to be more like him—thus perpetuating what is valued in this team and organization.

Melissa knows her customers inside out. She builds comprehensive growth plans for her accounts and dedicates herself to adding value to customers. On the team, she is seen as a pest because she is always complaining about the speed of

decision-making and response to customer needs. She has had great and not-so-great sales years, depending on how able she is to fulfill her promises to clients. During performance reviews she is seen as a solid performer but not outstanding, and many of her most positive attributes go undiscussed. Year after year she receives development feedback to be more transaction-oriented, like Ted.

One day, Ted and Melissa's manager is replaced. Initially, the new manager, Gladys, spends a lot of time trying to understand how her team has been delivering in the past. Because she most values customer feedback, Gladys works with Ted and Melissa specifically to hear about how each of them is serving their customers. With Ted, she detects the highly transactional nature of his work and the extent to which clients tolerate, but don't really like, him. Gladys immediately gives him some pointed feedback on his arrogance and expresses that this is not the kind of behavior that will win favor with her.

With Melissa it's the complete opposite. Her customers love her, but are frustrated with the company because they don't think her ideas and requests are adequately supported. Gladys spends long hours understanding Melissa's needs and dedicates herself to influencing the company to change their customer-facing approach. She also praises Melissa for her resilience, customer understanding, and openness to try new approaches.

Becoming a champion for the customers in her district, Gladys is able to support her team more effectively, but most especially Melissa, who becomes the most successful salesperson for that year. Meanwhile, Ted leaves the company to follow his previous manager.

Can you see how transforming what is valued can have a significant impact on performance? Ted was being overvalued for one contribution and not being properly assessed for the other: His negative impact on customers and the team. Melissa was being undervalued and not being properly assessed for her continuous push to make necessary changes to better serve customers.

Would you rather have a team of Teds or Melissas?

A team of Teds makes the manager look good. Numbers are delivered and all's right with the world – that is, until you dig deeper and see that this is not a team, but a loose collection of arrogant, boastful individuals working for their own ends.

A team of Melissas makes the manager work harder, because the manager has to actively support them in adding greater value to her customers. The end result of achieving the numbers may be exactly the same with each sales professional, but the process is drastically different.

But in the eyes of the customer, a team of Melissas is likely to represent the company's vision and mission far better than a team of Teds.

When managers value the process and behaviors as much as the end result, they build better professionals, more collaborative teams, and ultimately add more value to the customer—which should be the point of any business. This has nothing to do with being soft on people; rather, the point is to be more in tune with them. Possessing a deep knowledge of their capabilities, strengths, and potential derailers allows a servant leader to engage, motivate, and inspire the desired degree of performance more effectively. It is also a more demanding way to perform the job than even the higher-ups desire.

But servant leaders don't work for the higher-ups, they work solely for their people—to the pleasure or displeasure of senior leaders.

Another shift that managers need to make relates to shifting the psychology of performance away from weakness-fixing to talent-potentializing. This means becoming a talent scout, actively seeking those glimmers of brilliance in each collaborator. The focus moves away from short-term, numerical delivery toward long-term cultivation of potential. The reason this is crucial is highly rational, illustrated by the speed-reading example earlier: More energy is dispersed trying to develop weakness into strength than by taking strengths to the next level.

To demonstrate this, let's try an exercise together now.

Exercise

Pick up a pen and place it in your weaker hand. Then, write your full name ten times on a sheet of paper. Was that a pleasurable experience?
    What if I were to tell you that starting now, I only value people who

have perfect handwriting with both hands, and that I'm going to send you to handwriting courses to improve? Whenever you write with your strong hand I dismiss your performance, and when your off-hand scribing continues to suffer, I gripe and yell at you for not improving fast enough.

Do you want to continue working for me?

Now, write your name ten times with your strong hand.

Let's say I enroll you in a calligraphy class to take your handwriting to the next level. You are learning a new skill, building from an existing strength, and as you demonstrate new capabilities, I positively reinforce your progress and encourage you to keep developing. As you improve, I continuously challenge you to do more while supporting your growth.

How will our relationship feel at the end of your class?

The two elements of positive psychology

Positive psychology has two core elements, one simple and one more sophisticated. The first, simpler element deals with the energy that the manager puts out—their emotional impact on others. I call this the 'Positivity Quotient' (PQ). The second element relates to reinforcing strengths as the primary personal development focus. This is known as 'strengths-based leadership'—a phrase coined by Tom Rath in the book of the same name in 2009.[24]

Positivity Quotient

In a nutshell, PQ is a form of social intelligence that involves consciously applying positivity toward those around you to do the following:

- Enhance your own ability to influence productive outcomes

- Increase others' adherence to achieve their goals

Often, a manager's PQ is a key driver of employee engagement. Those with high PQ smile a lot, engage constantly, and reward progress regularly. They build stronger relationships with their employees, increase workplace productivity, and become better decision-makers because they inspire others to debate passionately for their causes.

Strengths-based leadership

Strengths-based leadership is based on trust, compassion, stability, and hope—the four values that Gallup found to be most desirable in leaders.[25]

In Chapter 3, we examined the importance of trust as the number one influence-builder (and thus, followership). However, compassion is hardly ever discussed as an important leadership value, despite the fact that it is extremely important in today's workforce. As known facts and ways of working are continuously disrupted by the volatile, uncertain, complex, and ambiguous nature of the world we live in today, having patience and compassion for forgivable mistakes and learning is essential, as is creating stability in this environment.

The 'Hedgehog Concept' in *Good to Great* states that the highest-performing companies have a core knowledge of what is most important regardless of the external environment, just as hedgehogs know how to do one thing brilliantly: roll into a ball of spikes whenever threatened. [26]

Lower-performing companies act more like foxes, constantly shifting tactics and approaches to achieve their goals. Stability comes when leaders declare what matters most over the long term and avoid knee-jerk reactions to short-term pressures.

Lastly, strengths-based leaders create hope for their people that all the investment these leaders make in their people will perpetually create more opportunities in the future. They paint a customer-focused vision of the future, where every employee can see how they fit in, and what they can contribute over the long term. When everything is going awry, creating hope that things can turn around is an invaluable asset, one that keeps productivity high and enhances retention of key talent.

When you combine PQ with the strengths-based leadership values of trust, compassion, stability, and hope, people will not only beat down doors to follow you—they will align, engage, and execute the mission more effectively over the long term.

Whether you are strengths-certified or not, focusing on your own impact on people, and ensuring that you walk the talk related to the attributes they most value, will transform your relationships and effectiveness.

Delivering effective feedback

But what about weakness? It can't just be allowed to proliferate like weeds in the sidewalk of the driveway, right? Well, since we now see that trying to develop a weakness into a strength is as futile as taking a calligraphy class with your weak hand, how can we make necessary improvements where we lack capability, or where derailing behaviors are prevalent?

The answer is feedback.

Once we value the correct aspects of performance beyond the numbers, desirable and undesirable behaviors in the culture will become obvious. Practitioners of positive psychology don't avoid giving constructive feedback: On the contrary, they need to be the most diligent providers and experts of this form of negative impact observation. Because they possess high PQ, they are highly sensitized to opposite behaviors—grumpiness, lack of engagement and collaboration, and arrogance. Beyond simply demonstrating their PQ daily, they influence others in the environment to adopt the same attributes by letting them know whenever they slip into negative states.

Because weakness can be expressed as the downside or unproductive application of an existing strength, managers must be in tune with employee strengths and understand when this is being expressed positively rather than negatively.

For example, I possess the strength of 'command.' This means I am unafraid of conflict, decisive, and generally have no problem taking charge in a crisis.

Over the years, my managers who have been aware of this strength have been great about rewarding me for applying it positively, such as making courageous decisions during a business crisis. However, they have also let me know when I was being unnecessarily combative or argumentative. Over time, I have learned to self-

modulate: Where command is not going to add value to a given situation, I simply don't use it.

The key in this example is the fact that my managers sought to understand first to potentialize my strengths, but also remained in tune with the downsides of these states: They constantly engaged me in increasing self-awareness, so I could calibrate and stay in my strengths zone.

This is the true benefit of investing in the Clifton Strengths Assessment for servant leaders. It helps them shift their mindset to value the how, as much as the what, behind performance objectives. It creates a framework through which to observe the employee, and creates a common language for feedback discussions, both positive and constructive. Lastly, it allows for potentialization of the entire team—which is what we will be looking at next!

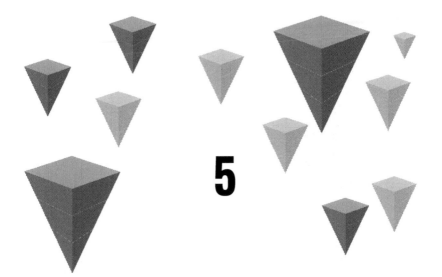

5

Focus on Your Team, Not Individual Talent

Let's recap. We have seen that the current form of leadership is incongruent with employees' needs in the *Leadership 3.0* era. As a result, a new style of motivating human performance is emerging that we call 'servant leadership.' This involves reorienting the top-down hierarchy to a more inclusive inverted hierarchy, where the people who serve the customer have the most important voices in the organization, and everyone else exists to serve and support them.

Those who wish to shift their leadership orientation first need to increase their personal effectiveness by adopting the behaviors of humility, intense will, and caring. Then, they need to learn how to increase their influencing skills, with or without authority, by demonstrating trust-building behaviors with all levels.

Positive psychology then becomes one of the major 'hows' of their style. By endeavoring to find what is right with people and help them find their strength zones, servant leaders potentialize performance faster and more sustainably than weakness-focused leaders. The key to mitigating weakness or derailing behaviors comes in the form of frequent, targeted feedback.

Still with me? Great!

Let's get into the more advanced skill set of a servant leader.

Forming and potentializing an expert team

Once a leader is oriented to a much broader group of stakeholders, rather than just to their bosses' wishes, they have to learn how to build and move teams through the stages of group development (as outlined in Chapter 1). But as with the other aspects of servant leadership, this requires another mindset shift away from the norms of *Leadership 2.0*: specifically, the notion that a few key talents can carry an organization to the promised land of continuous high performance.

As you will see, this is an archaic concept that no longer applies to the current business landscape.

The 'vitality curve' and why it doesn't work

I can't say exactly where the 'A Player' theory first emerged (A players being those talented few employees with the drive, capacity, and skills to change a company's fate). Perhaps it is a carryover from the military or sports. I first learned of this theory after reading Jack Welch's 2003 book *Jack: Straight From the Gut*, where he introduced the concept of the 'vitality curve.'[27] A vitality curve forces the employee base into a more insidious hierarchy, where A players make up the top 20%, B players approximately 70%, and C players the bottom 10%. Leaders who adopted this concept were encouraged to actively and rapidly promote the A players, tolerate the B players, and continuously remove C players from the organization.

This concept is quite seductive and well aligned with how we evaluate success in business in the west. However, it's also one of the key reasons for the employee disengagement crisis we are currently facing. It is also the complete opposite of servant leadership, in that it permits managers to take the easy way out, as opposed to assuming full responsibility for constructing and developing teams where the vast majority could qualify as A players in their own right. The very term 'A player' separates people who have to work together to achieve collective goals.

In my first people leadership role, at a company in Brazil, I implemented a vitality curve in my organization. I had inherited a relatively low-performing team and was tasked with reinvigorating the organization with talent and renewed purpose.

After a few training interventions, it was clear that the managers and most of my sales professionals were going to need much more time and investment to shift away from bad habits and poor discipline to become a high-performing team.

Rather than focus my efforts on those areas, I introduced a quarterly cut, where the bottom 10% of the sales team would be terminated without discussion. By the end of my first year in the position, we had expanded the organization but had terminated twenty-four collaborators-most of whom came from that original group.

We then used the headcount to bring in more 'A players.' And the results? We doubled sales in twelve months and tripled sales in two years, while expanding the organization from the original forty-two salespeople to 108 collaborators.

You're probably thinking to yourself at this point:

"Omar, what's the problem? The vitality curve worked, right?"

Well, actually, no it didn't. While the vitality curve certainly set the conditions for performance, it also became a source of extreme anguish for many in the organization who knew they were on the edge of entering the bottom 10%. Rather than inspiring performance, we were arbitrarily jettisoning people for nothing more than having a rough three months. Very few people can perform under that kind of pressure. But because I came up in the winner-takes-all corporate world of the U.S., I never considered the human carnage I was creating with my performance principles: I had basically built a team of mercenaries who would stop at nothing to remain in the 90%.

When I returned to Brazil in 2018, after ten years out of the market, the vast majority of my old team was still in the same roles as when I had led them. Now, I could certainly blame the marketplace, but I knew in my heart of hearts that the buck stopped with me.

I had invested very little time or energy in trying to understand the capabilities of each individual, beyond their talent for selling just enough not to get fired. And these people still upheld me as one of the best leaders for whom they had worked!

I was embarrassed, to say the least. I wished I could have gone back to 2006 and let the old me know there was a better way to accomplish the same objective.

But hindsight, as they say, is 20/20.

If I could go back in time, I would spend more time trying to understand the **why** behind my top performers' results and work to cascade this knowledge to all of the sales team. I would better leverage the top salespeople as trainers and champions, with the additional responsibility of evangelizing and energizing the rest of our team, so that everyone could enjoy the fruits of our labor.

I would have been far more cautious about terminating employees at the bottom of the sales rung without properly diagnosing and capitalizing on their full capability set. With that approach, maybe I would have quadrupled or quintupled sales in three years. Certainly, we would have created more leaders out of our crop of sales professionals than we did. And these leaders, in turn, would have been the catalysts for team performance, as they adopted and implemented servant leadership principles to cultivate the potential of each collaborator.

I am not at all supporting the position that key talent should not be highly prized by organizations or actively recruited, nurtured, stretched, and developed. What I am saying is that it is wholly insufficient and inefficient to base the fate of an organization on 20% of its population! It is lazy, offensive, and unintelligent to neglect to harness the entire potential existing within your human infrastructure. And for those arguing that it takes too much effort to do so, then I say: Cut 80% of your headcount, and see how well you deliver against your objectives for the time period being measured.

It costs way too much money to recruit, onboard, and train new employees, only to systematically abandon them because some measure of their performance or potential places them in the middle or bottom of the pack. Perhaps the way these people are being assessed needs to be rethought, or maybe the way they are being managed needs to be reinvented. No single person is more intelligent than a group of passionate, engaged, capable people.

Once you accept that the path to sustainable high performance lies in the team and not in one or two people, your approach to leadership is transformed for good.

You have to be the best version of yourself, both as a person and a leader, to coax achievement from a group with disparate temperaments, talents, and abilities. You have to work hard to connect with each individual, then bind them with each other. You have to derive your 'team DNA' and unleash it on your collective goals.

The benefits of this approach are clear. You can:

- Rely on the entire team's combined talent when setting objectives

- Lean on group wisdom to improve the quality of decision-making

- Recover from failure quickly, and scale success much faster

In short, you can win—together.

Focus on powering your team

This is where the real work begins, and where servant leaders outstrip their vitality curve- managing counterparts every time.

Servant leadership requires far greater capability and commitment, but it also delivers far more predictable and sustainable outcomes for the business. Working harder also equals working smarter, since the effort you put into cultivating a high-performance environment for a group of people ultimately pays significant dividends. It all begins with refocusing your attention away from key talent toward the composition of your team—the DNA of your collaborators.

I believe in this concept so much that I wrote a book dedicated to it called *Leader Board: The DNA of High Performance Teams.*[28] I will not recreate that work in the following sections; instead, I will dig deeper into the insights that drove me to this more holistic approach to team leadership, and how it fully aligns with the servant leaders' modus operandi.

Identify the endpoint

As mentioned previously, the servant leader increases employee engagement because she is actively involved with, and connected to, each individual collaborator and the team as a whole. She drives productivity by seeking to understand performance barriers at a fundamental level and dedicating herself to eliminating or navigating the organization around these barriers. She excels at retaining key talent because she knows who to empower, how to coach, and when to direct. And she does all of this while developing each person's innate capability, increasing their skills, and optimizing their impact.

Exceptional leaders are those who begin with the end in mind. They know where they are going, and what it will take to get there.

They intrinsically believe the phrase: 'If you want to go fast, go alone; but if you want to go far, go together.' It has taken the entirety of the human community to arrive at this place in history, so why do we believe, within companies, that a small group of people is all that is necessary to achieve the next leap in our journey? Perhaps it's creating a perception of scarcity that is more likely to lead to desired outcomes. When only a few select, ambitious (and often ruthless) people truly reap the benefits of everyone's collective effort, it behooves companies to identify these 'talents' early and satisfy their ambitions for more personal prestige and greater power.

Be an ethical leader

Society is set up to promote a winner takes all mentality – take our political elections process as an example. Even our modern definition of success is aligned with this paradigm, with an extremely small proportion of the human population possessing the vast majority of the resources—the top of the pyramid. However, this does not mean that these constructs are right. If they were, the world would not have devolved to such a state that humans are more concerned with the size of their followership and number of social media 'likes' than their impact on the environment.

Leadership 2.0 **has left the world morally bankrupt. And our children's children will bear the brunt of the burden.**

Consider this. Our politics of the moment are about power for the few at the expense of the needs of the many. In poll after poll, Americans make clear their extreme distrust and lack of belief that the government is working to serve their needs.[29] We know that our elected officials don't respond to us as much as they do to special interest groups and the billionaires controlling the purse strings.

When government orients itself away from the people it is designed to serve, revolution is not far behind—lest we forget the Arab Spring and similar movements sweeping around the world. The rhetoric of populism is seductive in this environment, because it promises a return of opportunity and shared prosperity to those who are demanding it most, by closing off borders, limiting globalization, and significantly raising the tensions of existing racial and class conflicts within the country's boundaries. At the end of the day, populism still concentrates power in the hands of even fewer nationalistic superiors, who think they know what is right for all the people—despots who respond to no one but their own ideals and delusions of grandeur.

This is a dangerous regression that we, the people, cannot allow to happen on our watch. And for those of us in positions of influence within our respective organizations, we can reverse the polarity of the status quo simply by focusing on the needs of the many instead of the few. This is more than just a better way to achieve results; it psychologically enables the concept that we are better and stronger together than apart.

Achieve success together, not alone

Individual brilliance will always be spotlighted in society. What is missed when we highlight these individual contributors is that while they are certainly talented in highly specific ways, even they could never have conquered their goals alone.

A great example of this is Alex Honnold, the first person to successfully scale El Capitan, a 3,000-foot vertical rock formation in Yosemite National Park, without the assistance of ropes—hence the term 'free soloing.'

As a climber, Alex is possessed of natural gifts-large hands and feet, lanky flexibility, core strength, formidable focus, determination, and self-assurance. When you watch the National Geographic documentary about him, **Free Solo**,[30] you become aware of Alex's team-his devoted girlfriend, an adventure performance coach in her own right, Sanni McCandless; his best friends and fellow climbers, Tommy Caldwell and Mark Synnott; and director Jimmy Chin. Although Alex ultimately initiates his climb unbeknown to his team, they assemble in time to document his brilliant achievement. In the aftermath of his accomplishment, he recognizes the crucial role that each of them played in getting him to the top safely, even if they couldn't make the climb with him.

Teams are the way forward. They are inclusive areas where everyone can contribute to constructing the path forward.

Teams are a space where there is equal opportunity to develop and explore individual and collective potential. They are the most consistent method of delivering continuous high performance.

What makes a team great?

Shared mission and purpose

Ultimately, team success depends on the group's ability to identify and focus on a clear and compelling performance challenge or common purpose. It can be a problem needing a solution. It can be an organizational goal. It can take many forms, but it is something that is clear and compelling to all team members. Importantly, everyone on the team understands that they are great at some things, and not so great at others.

Strong awareness of each other

Team members are aware of their unique talents, and how they can help the team respond to, or achieve, the performance challenge or goal. They also know how others on the team can best contribute. As such, they act interdependently.

They have an understanding of how each person is inclined to think, act, and feel. This awareness helps the team navigate the issues that all teams encounter. Certain talents make team members adept at managing conflict, documenting their work, setting direction, influencing others, etc. In short, they understand how the team can work best together.

The servant leader's role in forming a great team

The catalyst for this greatness is, of course, servant leadership. Servant leaders work diligently with their collaborators to define an inspiring cause that everyone responds to and works toward.

As outlined above, shared purpose is key: It is difficult to keep a group of people aligned, so establishing this early is of paramount importance. When leaders seek well-roundedness in individual contributors, they descend down the path of employee disengagement. Rather than seeking to be an inch thick and a mile wide with regard to capability, servant leaders should find people with a deep understanding of their true talents in a few areas, then learn how to best combine these synergistically, while leveraging other's peaks to cover their valleys. This is one of the best attributes of a high-performing team.

Servant leaders are also great promoters of diversity of talent, experiences, perspectives, and knowledge. Rather than forming homogeneous groups, they help heterogeneous collectives of people understand, acknowledge, and ultimately appreciate the value that comes with honoring, respecting, and leveraging each person's uniqueness.

Once again, this is a far more demanding job description than what is often expected of managers and leaders today. But just as ethics and compliance have dramatically shifted what is expected behaviorally of each employee, in a far more connected world that demands increasingly high standards of conduct, employee disengagement and the related fallout are likely to trigger a similar, dramatic shift in roles and norms—especially as these relate to a leader's responsibility set.

Adopt the team over individual talent ethos now, while the change is still simmering. If not, you could find yourself washed away in a tsunami of altered expectations.

Can I promise you that by following this principle you will deliver results faster in the short term than your more top-down-oriented contemporaries? No.

I won't even guarantee that your direct managers will acknowledge how hard you are working to create a cohesive, synergistic, aligned, and success-primed team. Remember: This manifesto is not about seeking the higher-ups' approval or recognition; it's about the people you were given the task to lead, guide, and develop. Their engagement level, individual and collective productivity, and loyalty to you and your organization are rewards in themselves.

When you focus on who is really on top—the team serving the customer—you begin to develop the focus needed to succeed in the game. This can lead to success not just in the finite game of quarterly targets and overly simplistic financial outcomes, but in the infinite pursuit of customer excellence, which we will look at next.

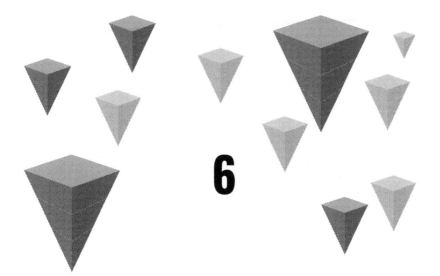

Perpetuating the Game: From Performance to Progress

I used to work with a senior executive who was fond of repeating the phrase:

"We exist at the pleasure of shareholders."

The clear implication was that if we didn't meet Wall Street's demands for constant growth without setbacks, we deserved to lose the trust of our 'owners.'

I found this to be a highly problematic philosophy for a leader of a so-called life sciences company dedicated (at least on paper) to helping people do more, feel better, and live longer. This mission only felt fully congruent if the people in question were rich, elite stockholders doing more by spending big with their annual dividends, living their best life on the spoils and efforts of the company's 100,000 or so employees, and extending their lives by having access to the best health care that money and influence can buy.

What's the right mission?

Surely, the missions of most health care companies are noble, motivating, and inspiring. I'm positive that if I were to interview researchers in the labs, folks in the product manufacturing department, or the sales representatives who dedicate their working hours to explaining the patient benefits of the company's medicines to health care professionals—all would speak of motives that directly align with the company's stated mission, vision, and values. Certainly, patients are benefiting from advances, not only in drug development, but also in the increasingly strategic ways that pharmaceutical companies go about ensuring broad access to these treatments by the people who truly need them. I only take issue with the notion that life sciences, health care, and pharmaceutical companies actually care as much about promoting health as much as they do about treating ailments and diseases.

As for-profit enterprises, these companies can't exist *only* to respond to patients' needs, right? They must make profits in a business that is increasingly competitive, highly regulated, and has enormous pressure on prices. This is forcing Big Pharma to achieve its public forecasts and targets by spiking prices wherever and whenever possible, cutting potential research and development programs, reducing employee headcount, lowering spend, averting taxes, and merging, partnering with, or acquiring other companies to gain scale, cost synergies, and accelerate pipeline progress.

Hang on—did you just read that correctly? Yes, you did.

I said that companies whose stated mission is to improve the lives of patients are seeking to do so by increasing the cost of the health care system, not contributing their fair share in taxes, and limiting future employment opportunities by diminishing the number of actual companies in existence. Where is all the supposed patient focus in these corporations' boardrooms? It's mostly nonexistent, because focusing on the long-term future of pharmaceutical science, innovation, and productivity is not rewarded by the majority of 'owners,' despite the clear understanding that the research and development pipeline is the lifeblood of any successful pharmaceutical company.

What if there were a health care company that understood their shareholders as merely investors, and positioned their 'owners' as the patients who consumed their products? Due to this enterprise's high connection with patient needs, trends, and opportunities, it looks to create solutions beyond medication to include monetizing health, instead of only offering treatments when people are diseased and feeling terrible about their outlook and condition.

Suppose it were to develop a novel cancer treatment-shouldn't it invest a similar amount in crafting solutions that can help people from ever developing the disease as it does in research and development, manufacturing, marketing, and sales?

Such a company could invest in public health education campaigns, raising awareness of environmental carcinogens and engaging in productive legal battles on patients' behalf to reduce controllable disease burden (i.e. lobbying against alcohol, fast food, and tobacco companies). It might focus as much on increasing the comfort related to its chemotherapy and radiation treatments as it does on getting the drugs approved and on the market. It might purchase or partner with integrative health companies to offer more holistic methods to patient care. It might focus on reducing the overwhelming medication burden that cancer patients face by creating safe product combinations for managing the known side effects of treatment.

How would the patients respond to such a company? I believe they would flock to its treatments. Cancer patients' families would rave about the degree of differentiated support that their loved ones received during treatment. They would be amazed at not only how well the company understands the disease, but also how much they care about patient well-being during the treatment process.

Would Wall Street reward such a company? Who cares! Creating customer value is the key to sustainable, long-term performance. In the Warren Buffett school of investment thinking, holding the right companies for the long haul nearly always results in significant wealth accumulation.

Still, many companies find themselves in this complex dilemma of courting investor satisfaction versus relentlessly pursuing a higher purpose or 'just cause'—but only one of these pursuits delivers employee engagement, productivity, and talent retention. If you guessed a higher purpose, give yourself a pat on the back. If you also guessed that servant leadership presents unique solutions to this dilemma, give yourself five gold stars!

The customer is eternal

If you were working for Ford in 1908, you would be selling Model Ts; 112 years later, you are selling Fusion hybrids. How many quarters have passed since the Model T's introduction? Approximately 448. Imagine the stress of trying to survive quarter-to-quarter for nearly 500 quarters or risk the ire of your shareholders!

Now, contrast that with trying to exceed customer needs and push the envelope on technology, safety, and performance—even if it means that some quarters are lower than desired, while others show explosive growth.

Remember: the people who serve the customer are precious.

Instead of rolling out annual sales objectives top-down, imagine building sales forecasts from the bottom up. First, by enabling line managers to analyze their business situation effectively, and second, by presenting a growth forecast that encompasses the necessary investment, strategies, tactics, and key measures of success.

When rolled all the way up, overall revenue projection might not be as ambitious as a forecast designed by the executive wing, but the level of engagement, commitment, and alignment will be far higher, resulting in more consistent and dependable growth rates. Employee rewards and recognition take on a different dimension, due to the augmented level of commitment to shared goals and focus on rewarding employees for resolving customer issues well, in addition to how many products they actually sell.

Profits should go further

Financial gain should come from delivering consistently excellent customer experience and ensuring that service employees are highly valued, engaged, and productive—not from filling investors' coffers. This furthers the journey to achieving a just cause.

Instead, investors should be encouraged to engage more actively with the company's cause and demonstrate their strategic alignment with its aims by walking the talk. Funding is easy; participating is harder. Infinite-minded investors are not only those who contribute for the long term; they also serve as the company's ambassadors, influencing others to join in on the cause, either via funding and services or recruiting the right people.

I am aware that all of this may sound a tad bit idealistic, and fully unreflective of the world we live in today. The fact is, I've spent twenty years operating in the real world, and have seen the negative side effects of profit chasing both in myself and those around me every day.

It wasn't until I read The Infinite Game by Simon Sinek[31] that I found the clear rationale behind my disgust. As Sinek explains, business has no end, but in deluded boardrooms and C- suites the world over, these incredibly smart people believe they can beat the system and win a game that is unwinnable by its very design.

Once I internalized this, the real problem behind the employee engagement crisis became readily apparent to me and gave rise to this manifesto.

Prioritize humanity

In a society where wealth is the defined as the accumulation of food, clothing, shelter, social status, and perceived safety, it makes some sense that people will attempt to achieve this stature via their company's market capitalization, how many people they hold dominion over, or how fast they can grow their personal nest eggs, regardless of the consequences. In many cases it's all three—and the sum result of this global chase is a small spike in serotonin levels, and a feeling in the pit of these individual's stomachs that there will always be someone younger, better, faster, or smarter coming for their paper throne.

Only by admitting, once and for all, that there is no winning in this game can we relieve ourselves of this false burden of importance and begin to realize our true potential as stewards of the game with one primary function: To perpetuate the game.

For example, just because tobacco grows on its own, can be tasty when smoked, and fulfills a demand for simple, handheld stress relief doesn't mean that it should be offered to people the world over, now that we understand that smoking is also responsible for mass death. How many Phillip Morris shareholders made billions during the cigarette smoking heyday, then turned around and castigated the company once it no longer became socially acceptable to light up wherever and whenever they desired?

It's time to remember our humanity—one of the central tenets of servant leadership.

There is no need for automatic assault weapons outside of the theater of war. We all know this, yet we allow gun manufacturers to prosper on the back of an antiquated constitutional amendment that does not reflect the world of today. It is obscene to think that some of the world's richest people are personally responsible for promoting policy and producing products with the sole purpose of eliminating life.

If you happen to be a line manager working for the Remington Arms Company on production of the 2021 array of death machines and are reading this book, I would ask you to take your talents for expert craftsmanship into a more life-affirming field. If you are a pricing manager at a pharmaceuticals company with a directive from the top to levy a massive price hike on your line of diabetes pens in 2020 before the next election cycle, anticipating that President Donald Trump may not win, please go to your customer service department and ask to speak with ten patients first, so as to understand the existing burden that your product's price is causing. Then, take that information back to the top and request a better way to achieve whatever arbitrary targets have been set.

Refuse apathy. Realize your impact on the world around you.

If you work for any company where senior management is out of touch with the customer; where they focus more on themselves than on cultivating passionate, knowledgeable employees; or where the only thing that matters is investor sentiment over actual societal impact—my advice to you, whether you're working in a line management or individual contributor role, is to seek a better environment.

For when the finite results don't come in, who will be at risk of losing everything?

You, not the executive branch. There are no golden parachutes for middle management, just the minimum severance required by law… and some weak job transition counseling.

Shift the perception of 'performance'

The litmus test here is simple. If the product, service, or solution truly serves a need, and producing it doesn't endanger its intended users, environment, or the people making it, then it should be produced, promoted, and profited upon.

The next step up is to leverage these well-deserved profits into improving the lives of the product's intended users, producers, and the communities where the corporation operates. The people producing it should be encouraged, coached, and inspired to do more at work and in their lives outside the office. And the customer should be encouraged by the product or service to do more, be more, and maximize their positive impact on the world around them.

Why patience is crucial

The key concept here is one that does not get acknowledged enough in the business world: Patience. When the purpose of the game is to perpetuate it, patience becomes of paramount importance. Patience to remain steadfast to the just cause, no matter what the short-term results demonstrate. Patience to cultivate excellent culture, products, people, and processes. Patience to actively listen to customers, understand their needs on a deep level, and gain insights that enable the company to serve them for years to come.

Exactly how does a servant leader perpetuate the game?

By redefining performance as progress.

Over an infinite time span, the sales achievements of any given year become less significant than the years where major progress toward the just cause was made. Long-term performance is nothing more than an ability to stimulate continuous positive progress and sustained momentum. As such, progress cannot be measured in sales figures alone—it needs to include the impact on the customer, the community, and the company's people.

Take Apple, for example. It's not every year that it reinvents the status quo by launching a game- changing innovation like the iPhone or iPad.

At the same time, judging Apple on the volume of sales of iPhones and iPads doesn't tell you how much progress the company has made during a calendar year. Not even a trillion-dollar valuation can calculate the total size of Apple's contributions to society, communities, and its internal contributors.

However, under an infinite context, even Apple has major work to do to repair its reputation, due to its predatory labor practices in China. This should be a point of major loss of organizational pride and engagement for a company that literally empowers millions of people to achieve their dreams via forced obsolescent technology.

Apple chased finite profits and lost its soul in the process. Don't let the same happen on your watch.

How to measure progress

Within this context, a servant leader has to expand how they evaluate progress. Achieving sales targets set by someone else is not progress—it's merely effort, and sometimes luck. Individual strengths development might count as progress only to the degree that the individual in question has learned how to leverage their strengths for the good of the team that serves the customer. Making the time to do good in the community is just as important for progress as the number of hours working on key commercial projects. And measuring the impact of the work on the customer is crucial, both to accelerate the journey and achieve more of those milestone years.

Find a company with an infinite mindset—they exist, believe me.

Invest in becoming a more holistic leader.

Holistic leadership requires the right degree of work ethic, heart, optimism, and maturity (W.H.O.M.).[32] If you don't possess the W.H.O.M. you desire today, improving here is your first step. The degree of W.H.O.M. in the team (and in you, as its leader) determines what will be possible, and how quickly. This is because teams today require more than just direction to succeed. They require the intangible aspect of love, which is where servant leadership truly reinvents the game.

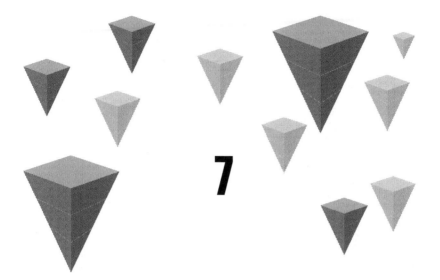

7

Lead with Love

Fact: People's needs don't change once they walk through the office door—their motivations, desires, and requirements become no less intense or important. And because so many corporations serve a noble purpose, it is surprising just how little of the higher-order needs of humanity are served by the work we do, and with whom we do it.

Obviously, there is something missing here.

In his seminal work on a unified theory of human motivation, psychologist Abraham Maslow introduced the concept of a hierarchy of needs (Figure 2).[33] This progressive pyramid begins with the most basic human requirements—food, clothing, and shelter—and moves ever upward to the peak of self-actualization, where altruism, morality, problem-solving, and acceptance of facts become requirements for continued growth and motivation.

MASLOW'S HIERARCHY OF NEEDS

Figure 2: Maslow's hierarchy of needs.
Source: DepositPhotos.com (Standard license, reproduced with permission)

Interestingly enough, if we apply Maslow's hierarchy of human needs to the top-down management hierarchy in place in most organizations today (Figure 3), it reveals a tremendous disconnect.

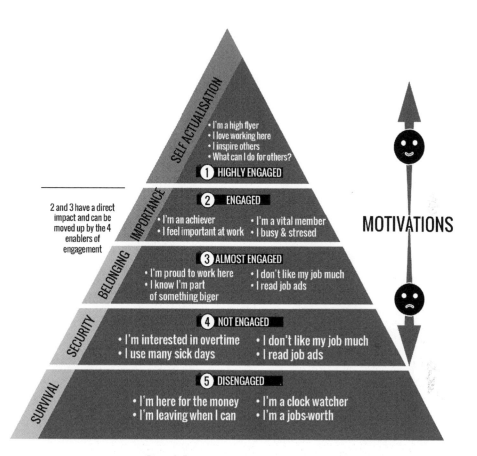

Figure 3: Employee engagement hierarchy.

Not all leaders are role models

Often, senior leaders are not models of altruism, morality, problem-solving, and acceptance of facts within corporations or society at large. In fact, they are frequently egocentric, corrupt, problem-creating, and fact-denying. Their lack of self-actualization trickles down throughout the organization, actively stifling others' self-actualization until the entire enterprise becomes locked into a rat race, with individuals chasing the accumulation of lower-order needs—status and style over substance and real impact. Still, Maslow's hierarchy cannot be denied. Humans need self-actualization for full engagement with life as much as we need water. The only difference is a lack of water causes physical death, but a lack of self-actualization causes spiritual death.

Why aren't those in charge of enterprises held to the highest standards of human behavior?

Is there something inherently wrong with the theory of human motivation, capitalism, or humans ourselves?

Is it laziness or lack of knowledge that prevents us from holding those in charge accountable for the active and conscious cascading of opportunities that only self-actualization provides?

Or is it because we have accepted this void in our own set of needs? Much like choosing to eat fast food while being fully aware that more fulfilling and enriching nutritional options are available.

Maybe, we just don't know what we don't know. If we haven't been exposed to self-actualized leaders on a mass scale, our collective expectation of our leaders is far lower than it should be. For every Mahatma Gandhi throughout history, there are literally thousands of maniacal tyrants destroying the world for the accumulation of perceived power.

This is why in order to change the status quo, we must become the change we want to see in the world.

Senior leaders are not changing their spots anytime soon—but they can, and will, be replaced by a new guard. It is my sincere hope that this new guard will be mostly made up of servant leaders.

Don't wait for the call: Become your best self now

As good parents, we are at our most self-actualized. We ignore our own needs to provide for our offspring: We sleep less, eat less, and become less focused on our own egos. We focus on nurturing and providing for others, oftentimes at our own expense. We do this because within most of us there is a biological command directing us to do so. Parents are natural servant leaders. Corporations are littered with parents. So why are we dropping our nurturing instincts as soon as we pass through the office door? Why are we allowing the corporate environment to prevent us from being our best selves?

It's because we are waiting for the command to come down from on high to direct us to do so—a command that is never going to come from hierarchy-clinging, *Leadership 2.0* stalwarts. We have to empower ourselves to change the pecking order for our people, even if it doesn't result in immediate recognition or instant gratification. Parenthood is a slog—but we commit because what we derive from it is a feeling of peace and love unrivaled in human experience. When we serve our children, we are filled with light, inspiration, creativity, and possibility.

As discussed in the previous chapters of this book, the toolbox of an effective servant leader is filled with:

- Proactivity

- Humility

- Intense personal will

- High-performance habits

- Strong discipline

- Caring

- Trust-building behavior

- Positive psychology

- Well-developed team management skills

- Extreme patience
- A progress-equals-performance approach

If you compare this list of attributes to a great parent or effective coach, you will see a great deal of overlap. Still, there is one tool missing—the hammer of the toolbox as it were—and this is love. Not the love you find in wedding vows: Servant leaders understand love as both a reason and an action.

Ikigai is the Japanese concept of synthesizing your reason for living, life purpose and source of endurance (Figure 4).[34]

Figure 4: The ikigai philosophy

Source: Standard license Adobe Stock (reproduced with permission)

Ikigai combines passion, mission, profession, and vocation to identify the sweet spot that each of us should be working to define and achieve. Have you ever asked yourself the following questions?

- What do I love?

- What am I good at?

- What can I be paid for?

- What can I contribute to the world?

Certainly, answering these crucial questions and refining your responses over time will lead to a more productive and exhilarating life—but only to the degree that you can calibrate and balance the responses. We have all been in love with something at which we weren't necessarily the best. We have all been good at something that we didn't necessarily appreciate. We have all been paid for something at which we weren't necessarily that good. We all have causes that we want to be a part of, but shy away from fully participating in, because it might not pay the bills.

How do we obtain harmony between all these aspects? One way is through the lens of love, because love is the unifying factor intrinsic in each facet of *ikigai*. There are five types of love that can accelerate your path toward *ikigai*, once you fully understand and harmonize them.

Self-love

This is about being a healthy human: Mind, body, and soul. Nothing in life can be achieved without health, so this aspect is the bedrock of *ikigai*. Consistency and discipline are the keys to self-love. You need plenty of sleep, the right fuel, space for reflection, and, if appropriate, spiritual guidance on your quest for fulfillment, so make sure this area is prioritized.

Interest love

Healthy people have multiple interest areas, and a genuine curiosity about life and living. Pay attention to the things that pique this, as they can grow to become the activities that inspire and energize you. Making time to pursue your interests and increase your knowledge will help you keep your outlook positive and progressive. (And who knows, that hobby or interest might become lucrative someday.)

Purpose love

When areas of personal inspiration align with your natural talent, you are on the path to achieving your purpose. The energy of inspiration coupled with the power of your unique abilities can make you an unstoppable force—as long as you put in the work necessary to refine these talents into reliable strengths.

Being intentional is the key. Don't ignore the areas of natural uniqueness that you possess. Embrace these 'spikes of specialty,' then work to become the absolute best version of yourself.

Team love

On your path to your purpose, you are likely to meet others who share similar inspiration and complementary talents to your own. By joining forces, you can achieve more than either of you could accomplish alone.

Your team doesn't just mean the people that work alongside you. It also includes those who cheer you on, console you when you are down, watch your back, and provide valuable mentorship, coaching, and advice. The most important aspect of choosing your team is ensuring that they energize and support you, rather than drain and reject you (and you willingly do the same). Without team love, most purpose remains just a distant dream.

Financial love

With health, knowledge, purpose, and community, you can be considered a wealthy person already. If you've combined the above four elements, it is highly unlikely that you will be dissatisfied with how well you are being compensated.

However, financial choices can either constrain or free us, so financial love is about how well you leverage income from your career and other pursuits to feel secure enough to keep dreaming and doing. Spending less than you make, saving as much as you can, and planning for unforeseen events and retirement are all demonstrations of financial love. In this way you are neither 'living to work' nor 'working to live'—you are simply financially stable, secure, and satisfied.

Ikigai as a leadership model

Pursuit of *ikigai* and these sources of love gives us direct guidance on how to lead ourselves, our families, and our people.

The reason employees are disengaged is because managers are disengaged.

Managers are disengaged because senior leaders are disengaged.

Senior leaders are disengaged because investors are disengaged.

It's a doom spiral: Wrong values lead to wrong behaviors, which lead to wrong measures, which leads to poor outcomes for customers, the community, and internal collaborators. By the measure of *ikigai*, few people are winning at life, and much less so at the infinite game of business. Money and financial resources only complete one of three requisites—and if you are not being paid for what you are good at, what the world needs, and/or what you love to do, what is the point?

Don't choose misery, because misery loves company. This is why today's companies are failing to offer to employees true fulfillment in their lives.

Love is the key to flipping the status quo on its head and creating a hierarchy that nurtures the best of humanity, rather than juicing humans like the machines in *The Matrix*. If each of us can dedicate ourselves to the pursuit of the five types of love listed above, only then can we help others achieve their own five sources of love.

Love begets love—and when actively leveraged, love transforms lives.

Imagine a workplace where people are not only encouraged, but required, to invest in themselves in this way. Will more fulfilled individuals be better or worse customer stewards, teammates, or leaders?

Now, think about how you are leading your team.

- What activities and pursuits are you valuing?
- What type of example are you setting?
- What needs are you opting not to satisfy?

Any personal development plan that does not contemplate human needs beyond a corporate framework will fail to deliver the types of employees that can carry the company forward. Vitality curves are unnecessary when each employee is seen as a viable, valuable, and vital contributor to the just cause. Financial rewards and the accumulation of status symbols pale in comparison to the rewards of true actualization, of one's *ikigai*. Wall Street crumbles in the face of an organization that knows and owns its role in the world as a source of inspiration, creativity, problem-solving, and altruism. Quarterly targets dissipate against the gale-force winds of human progress and possibility.

All fueled by love.

By nature, servant leaders put the mission and people before their own needs.

They do this, not out of some masochistic desire to suffer, but because they have realized that by giving of themselves, they get far more back in return. They are the true investors of the business world, because they come to work every day and invest in cultivating the human potential around them. They work only in service of the mission, their people, and ultimately, the customer. And in return, they reap the higher-order benefits of self-actualization—greater fulfillment and engagement with their own lives, further progress toward their goals and objectives, and more frequent, higher-value achievements to boost their esteem and ego.

That's the power of love. It's the only thing that returns double what was initially invested.

Like the intern whom you take the time to mentor in their natural strengths.

Or the struggling collaborator whom you work with to understand and appreciate their natural way of thinking, feeling, or behaving.

Or the agile, restless teammate whom you inspire to spend as much time sharing best practices as chasing financial rewards and status.

Or the disengaged person whom you help to diagnose the source of their unhappiness and get on the path toward greater fulfillment.

Or the team that struggles to cohere, until you help them air out their grievances, build trust, and form productive norms.

Or the division that you course correct by changing what is valued and aligning the work with customer needs.

Or the company that you transform into a beacon of progress by combining the *ikigai* of thousands of collaborators into a just cause that inspires the world to be a better place.

Servant leaders can do all of this and more for themselves, their families, their teams, and their organizations. By loving themselves enough to not be satisfied by the accumulation of lower-order needs, they make it okay for others to make the same choice. And this pursuit of the love that drives us to be the best for both ourselves and those around us can only result in higher engagement, increased productivity, and competitive advantage in talent retention.

But it all starts with having the courage to fully commit to your own personal pursuit of *ikigai*.

Want to put the lessons of this book in practice? Start by building a plan to fulfill the five sources of love for yourself.

Then, when you are ready, give the same gift to your people. Watch the seeds that you plant grow into a veritable forest of positivity, possibility, and progress.

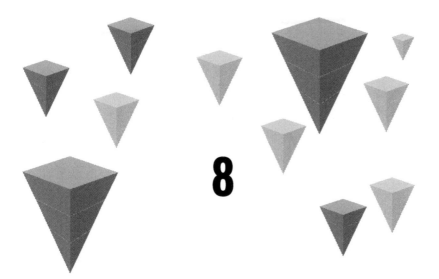

8

The Servant Leader's Learning Journey

At this point, I'm sure you're convinced that servant leadership is the solution to a global engagement crisis—a crisis that stems from applying archaic management practices to a generation of workers where team collaboration, technological proficiency, and diversity are the hallmarks of the age.

It's also totally understandable if you still have questions. My ask here is pretty big, so it's completely relatable if you want more information before you join our tribe! Each section of this book comes backed up with many years of copious reading and research into the topic by me, as well as some of the greatest management science luminaries.

Let's dive in!

Introduction

The ideas in this section in terms of *Leadership 1.0 to 3.0* are of my original conception. However, there are many management science books about the construction of the top-down hierarchy during the Industrial Revolution and during the post–Korean War economic boom in the U.S. (I'm aware that I massively oversimplify the description of the major influences and trends in these periods—not to suit my argument, but to streamline the discussion.) To a large extent, Adam Smith's *The Wealth of Nations*[35] informs the *Leadership 1.0* argument.

The demographic argument at the start of *Leadership 2.0* can be defended by census and employee data from the 1950s through the 1990s.[36] Programs such as 'affirmative action' created significant white-collar workforce access for African Americans.[37] Women faced a much tougher journey, from having access to only limited role scopes to holding senior leadership roles in Fortune 500 companies. *The Innovators* by Walter Isaacson[38] informed the section on how the emergence of technology transformed the way that work was done, at the same time as the face of the workforce was shifting.

Books such as *First, Break All the Rules* by Jim Harter and Markus Buckingham;[39] *Good to Great* by Jim Collins;[40] *How Full is Your Bucket?* by Donald O. Clifton and Tom Rath,[41] *Strengthsfinder 2.0*[42] and *Strengths-Based Leadership*[43] by Tom Rath, *The Servant: A Simple Story of the True Essence of Leadership* by James C. Hunter[44] and *Start with Why* by Simon Sinek[45] all deeply examine the state of the modern workforce at the turn of the century, and elucidate the disconnect between senior management and the employee base.

When you read these works, you clearly see the trend of team over individual talent emerging, even as the positive psychology and company vision–based movements begin to offer a new approach to engaging these new employee types. While these works don't explicitly point at servant leadership as the solution to the employee engagement crisis, Ron Friedman's *The Best Place to Work*[46] and Jim Clifton and Jim Harter's *It's The* Manager,[47] come closest to empirically calling for radical transformation in team leadership.

What Is Servant Leadership?

In the early 1970s, Robert Greenleaf coined the term 'servant leadership.'[48] I first learned the term 'servant leader' by reading *The*

Servant. Greenleaf's first work on the topic was published in 1977, at a time when the world was still quite entrenched in the *Leadership 2.0* era, so he was definitely way ahead of the curve. Other treatments of the subject can be found in Ken Blanchard's *The Servant Leader*[49] and John C. Maxwell's *The 21 Irrefutable Laws of Leadership,*[50] *Developing the Leader Within You 2.0*, and Tom Rath and Donald O. Clifton's *How Full is Your Bucket?*[51]—all of these delve deeply into the need for leaders to embrace this concept.

For empirical proof of the merits of servant leadership, you need to get into *Good to Great.* Collins changes the 'servant leader' nomenclature to 'Level 5 leadership,' but essentially the message remains the same. The most successful companies are led by leaders who possess humility and deep personal will—two defining attributes of servant leadership. In this case, success is measured simply by stock performance over a thirty-year period. Companies led by servant leaders delivered on average ten times better shareholder returns than their comparators in the same industries.

I strongly recommend you read these books, as they will certainly provide plenty of food for thought on top of this manifesto.

How to Manifest Personal Effectiveness

Three books form the backbone of this principle: *The 7 Habits of Highly Effective People* by Stephen Covey,[52] *The Miracle Morning* by Hal Elrod,[53] and *An Astronaut's Guide to Life on Earth* by Colonel Chris Hadfield.[54] The higher up I have progressed as a leader in my career, the more I have observed a strong correlation between my degree of personal effectiveness and my ability to be my best for my team. It occurred to me that people have a habit of mimicry: They tend to copy the leaders they admire. If I wanted to embed servant leadership principles in my organization—more than just being consistent in the office—I needed to increase that consistency in every area of my life.

I was already leveraging Stephen Covey's first habit religiously in terms of keeping my team and organization focused on what we could control, but I realized that I wasn't yet acting on every area within my control. I wasn't attacking my bad habits. I wasn't actively pursuing my best self in every arena of my life. Then I discovered *The Miracle Morning* and everything changed. This book exists in no small degree because of the habits I began implementing while and after reading Hal Elrod's highly motivating book. Once I took to waking up earlier, sleeping a bit less, hydrating better, exercising more, practicing affirmations, meditating, reading, journaling, writing, and visualizing every single day, I felt connections beginning to fire in my mind that had never occurred previously. I even made a link to a book I had read back in 2018 by Col. Hadfield, which spoke about the level of preparation, discipline, and collaboration of some of the smartest and bravest people on Earth and in space.

Put it all together: To serve others, first you must serve yourself—but not the ego. If you are giving yourself what you need to self-actualize and achieve *ikigai*, you will no longer look to a corporation or boss authority figure to do anything for you. You can focus on you and those in your charge and leave the worrying to others.

Use Influence, Not Authority

When I was young in my career, before I had ever led a team, I read John C. Maxwell's *The 21 Irrefutable Laws of Leadership*. The very first law—the 'law of the lid'—had always stymied me. Collins defines leadership as influence right from the outset, and he states that you can only influence others who are below your leadership capability: His concept is that acquiring leadership capability is the most important way to augment organizational influence. This sounded like the kind of thing that looked good in a book but had little relevance in the real world.

Years later, I was appointed general manager of a global multinational pharmaceutical company's operations in Indonesia, leading an enterprise of 700 people. As I navigated the myriad challenges of my new position, I became aware that my lid was not high enough because I was struggling to get my team to cohere and perform. I needed to learn much more, much faster—so I revisited all my leadership gurus' work until I was able to innovate the Team Performance Acceleration Principles (TPAPs) at the heart of my book *Leader Board: The DNA of High Performance Teams*.[55]

James C. Hunter also talks extensively about the power of seeking influence over authority in *The Servant*, and Patrick Lencioni's *The Five Dysfunctions of a Team* provides a good example of how a leader can influence their team better through the dysfunctional storming phase.[56] More importantly, more than fifteen years of implementing servant leadership principles has shown me the power of influence.

How to Leverage Positive Psychology for Success

How Full is Your Bucket? is the bible of positive psychology for me. The author, Donald O. Clifton, invented the term from his investigation of what made successful people tick, back in the 1960s. Clifton purchased the Gallup organization in the early 1980s and turned it into a global force for driving organizational change backed up by empirical data and sound advice. Clifton's work resulted in the 'bucket-filling' philosophy and tactics implemented by servant leaders, as well as the strengths-based leadership movement, kicked off by Clifton and Markus Buckingham's *Now Discover Your Strengths*[57] in 2001 and continuing with Tom Rath's *Strengthsfinder 2.0* and *Strengths-Based Leadership* in 2006 and 2009. The consolidation of all these practices can be found in *It's the Manager* by Jim Clifton and Jim Harter of Gallup.

The point Gallup makes is clear: When employees discover and develop their strengths instead of focus on weakness, and receive high-performance coaching at all levels of management (Gallup's term for servant leadership), the transformation in employee engagement, productivity, and retention of key talent is astounding. As simple as this sounds, it is much harder to implement in practice—which is why Chapter 2 on personal effectiveness in this book is so fundamental. If you as leader are not in a good space, your efforts to cascade positivity and develop strengths in your organization are likely to fall flat.

The empirical impact of positive psychology is well explored also in *Emotional Intelligence 2.0* by Travis Bradberry and Jean Greaves.[58]

As a Gallup Certified Strengths coach and someone who has implemented positive psychology and strengths-based leadership at the enterprise level, I can personally attest to how much more meaningful my relationships have become with my direct reports, and how much more quickly I have been able to help them develop and accelerate their careers.

When your people know that you truly have their best interests at heart, when you gain access to what genuinely motivates and inspires them, and when you build them up rather than tearing them down, the results speak for themselves.

Focus on Your Team, Not Individual Talent

If you are curious about the 'vitality curve' concept, I highly recommend you read Jack Welch's *Jack: Straight from the Gut*[59] as the example of what not to do. I return to Jim Collins' teachings in his books *Good to Great* and *Great by Choice*,[60] which link how teams are needed to progress in today's age. In *Good to Great,* this is defined as 'First Who, Then What'—meaning getting the right people in the organization before deciding where to aim your ambitions. Also, do read Walter Isaacson's Steve Jobs biography[61] to learn the dark side of Jobs' obsession with 'A players,' and the resulting chaos and rampant disengagement.

Other strong arguments for this principle can be found in *The Best Place to Work* by Ron Friedman, *The Ideal Team Player* by Patrick Lencioni,[62] and *The 17 Essential Qualities of a Team Player* by John C. Maxwell.[63] Each of these books, in their own ways, recognize the power of teams and the need for leaders to evolve better team leadership skills. I am biased, but the most comprehensive book on this subject may just be my own: *Leader Board: The DNA of High Performance Teams.*

Perpetuating the Game: From Performance to Progress

This chapter was directly inspired by *Start With Why* and *The Infinite Game* by Simon Sinek.[64] After reading Sinek's latest book, a fire was lit in my soul. I had to speak on this topic—because finite-mindedness (a hallmark of *Leadership 2.0*) is ruining the world. If you want to be doubly fired up, I suggest you pick up *The Infinite Game* immediately!

Lead with Love

The primary reading for this section comes from *Maslow on Management* by Abraham H. Maslow,[65] and *Ikigai: The Japanese Secret to a Long and Happy Life* by Héctor García and Francesc Miralles.[66] Maslow connected his hierarchy of human needs to business success way back in 1965! He made the connection between self-actualization and high-performance culture before this was even a thing. If you read no other books I reference in this section, please read these two. You will come out the other side positively transformed and ready to improve not only your own life, but the lives of everyone around you.

If each of us does our part, the status quo will change. Other books, such as *Wellbeing: The Five Essential Elements* by Tom Rath[67] and *Thrive: The Third Metric to Redefining Success and Creating a Life of Well-Being, Wisdom, and Wonder* by Arianna Huffington,[68] are more modern takes on the same principle.

References

Introduction

1   Gallup.com. 'Building a high-development culture through your employee engagement strategy.' www.gallup.com/workplace/285800/development-culture-engagement-paper-2019.aspx, February 21, 2020.

2   Jim Clifton and Jim Harter. *It's the Manager: Gallup Finds the Quality of Managers and Team Leaders is the Single Biggest Factor in Your Organization's Long-Term Success.* Gallup Press, 2019.

3   Patrick Reams and Ruán Magan. *The Men Who Built America.* The History Channel, 2013.

4   History.com editors. 'Women's suffrage.' www.history.com/topics/womens-history/the-fight-for-womens-suffrage, October 11, 2019.

5   Margot Lee Shetterly. *Hidden Figures: The American Dream and the Untold Story of the Black Women Mathematicians Who Helped Win the Space Race.* William Morrow Paperbacks, 2016.

6   Pew Research Center. 'The American middle class is losing ground.' www.pewsocialtrends.org/2015/12/09/the-american-middle-class-is-losing-ground/, December 9, 2015.

7   Bailey Reiners. '80+ Diversity in the workplace statistics you should know.' https://builtin.com/diversity-inclusion/diversity-in-the-workplace-statistics, November 6, 2019.

Chapter 1: What is Servant Leadership?

8 Donald O. Clifton and Tom Rath. *How Full is Your Bucket?* Gallup Press, 2004.

9 Patrick Lencioni. *The Five Dysfunctions of a Team: A Leadership Fable.* Jossey-Bass, 2003.

10 John C. Maxwell. *The 21 Irrefutable Laws of Leadership: Follow Them and People Will Follow You.* Thomas Nelson, 2007.

11 Jim Collins. *Good to Great: Why Some Companies Make the Leap and Others Don't.* Harper Business, 2001.

12 Simon Sinek. *Start With Why: How Great Leaders Inspire Everyone to Take Action.* Penguin Group, 2009.

13 Robert K. Greenleaf. 'The servant as leader.' The Greenleaf Center for Servant Leadership, 1970.

14 Gallup. 'Q12 Assessment.' www.gallup.com/access/239210/employee-engagement-survey.aspx

15 Bruce W. Tuckman. 'Developmental sequence in small groups.' Psychological Bulletin, 1965, Vol. 63, No. 6, 386–387.

16 Rob Peters. 'Why the key to management is getting rid of the managers.' Medium.com. https://medium.com/@standardoftrust/why-the-key-to-management-is-getting-rid-of-the-managers-1f4852daab87, November 19, 2018.

Chapter 2: How to Manifest Personal Effectiveness

17 Walter Isaacson. *Steve Jobs.* Simon & Schuster, 2011.

18 Jim Collins. *Good to Great: Why Some Companies Make the Leap and Others Don't.* Harper Business, 2001. pp. 21–22.

19 Isaacson, *Steve Jobs.*

20 Stephen R. Covey. T*he 7 Habits of Highly Effective People: Powerful Lessons in Personal Change.* Mango Publishing Group, 1989.

21 Simon Sinek. *Find Your Why: A Practical Guide for Discovering Purpose for You and Your Team.* Portfolio, 2017.

Chapter 4: How to Leverage Positive Psychology for Success

22 Clifton StrengthsFinder themes. Copyright © 2000, 2012 Gallup, Inc. All rights reserved. Gallup®, StrengthsFinder, Clifton StrengthsFinder, and each of the 34 Clifton StrengthsFinder theme names are trademarks of Gallup, Inc.

23   J.W. Glock. 'The relative value of three methods of improving reading: Tachisoscope, films, and determined effort.' Ph.D. thesis, University of Nebraska-Lincoln, 1955.

24   Tom Rath. *Strengths-Based Leadership: Great Leaders, Teams, and Why People Follow*. Gallup Press, 2009.

25   Rath, *Strengths-Based Leadership*, p. 82.

26   Jim Collins. *Good to Great: Why Some Companies Make the Leap and Others Don't.* Harper Business, 2001, p. 90.

Chapter 5: Focus on Your Team, Not Individual Talent

27   Jack Welch with John A. Byrne. *Jack: Straight from the Gut*. Grand Central Publishing, 2003, p. 71.

28   Omar L. Harris. *Leader Board: The DNA of High Performance Teams*. The Pantheon Collective, 2018.

29   Lee Rainie and Andrew Perrin. 'Key findings about Americans' declining trust in government and each other.' Pew Research Center. www.pewresearch.org/fact-tank/2019/07/22/key-findings-about-americans-declining-trust-in-government-and-each-other/, July 22, 2019.

30   Free Solo, dir. Elizabeth Chai Vasarhelyi and Jimmy Chin, documentary, National Geographic, 2018.

Chapter 6: Perpetuating the Game: From Performance to Progress

31   Simon Sinek. *The Infinite Game*. Penguin Group, 2019.

32   Omar L. Harris. *Leader Board: The DNA of High Performance Teams*. The Pantheon Collective, 2018, p. 14.

Chapter 7: Lead with Love

33   Abraham Maslow. *Toward a Psychology of Being*. Martino Fine Books, 1962.

34   Héctor García and Francesc Miralles. *Ikigai: The Japanese Secret to a Long and Happy Life*. Penguin Books, 2017.

Chapter 8: The Servant Leader's Learning Journey

35   Adam Smith. *The Wealth of Nations*. Coterie Classics (reprint edition), 2016[1776].

36   Mitra Toossi. 'A century of change: The U.S. labor force, 1950–2050.' Monthly Labor Review, May 2002.

37 Terry H. Anderson. *The Pursuit of Fairness: A History of Affirmative Action*. Oxford University Press, 2004.

38 Walter Isaacson. *The Innovators: How a Group of Hackers, Geniuses, and Geeks Created the Digital Revolution*. Simon & Schuster, 2014.

39 Jim Harter and Markus Buckingham. *First Break All the Rules: What the World's Greatest Managers Do Differently*. Gallup Press, 2016.

40 Jim Collins. *Good to Great: Why Some Companies Make the Leap and Others Don't*. Harper Business, 2001.

41 Donald O. Clifton and Tom Rath. *How Full is Your Bucket? Positive Strategies for Work and Life*. Gallup Press, 2004.

42 Tom Rath. StrengthsFinder 2.0. Gallup Press, 2013.

43 Tom Rath. *Strengths-Based Leadership: Great Leaders, Teams, and Why People Follow*. Gallup Press, 2009.

44 James C. Hunter. *The Servant: A Simple Story About the True Essence of Leadership*. Random House, 2008.

45 Simon Sinek. *Start With Why: How Great Leaders Inspire Everyone to Take Action*. Penguin Group, 2009.

46 Ron Friedman. *The Best Place to Work: The Art and Science of Creating an Extraordinary Workplace*. TarcherPerigee, 2014.

47 Jim Clifton and Jim Harter. *It's the Manager: Gallup Finds the Quality of Managers and Team Leaders is the Single Biggest Factor in Your Organization's Long-Term Success*. Gallup Press, 2019.

48 Robert K. Greenleaf. 'The servant as leader.' The Greenleaf Center for Servant Leadership, 1970.

49 Ken Blanchard. *The Servant Leader*. Thomas Nelson, 2003.

50 John C. Maxwell. *The 21 Irrefutable Laws of Leadership: Follow Them and People Will Follow You.* Thomas Nelson, 2007.

51 John C. Maxwell. *Developing the Leader Within You 2.0*. HarperCollins Leadership, 2018.

52 Stephen R. Covey. *The 7 Habits of Highly Effective People: Powerful Lessons in Personal Change*. Mango Publishing Group, 1989.

53 Hal Elrod. *The Miracle Morning: The Not-So-Obvious Secret Guaranteed to Transform Your Life (Before 8AM)*. Miracle Morning Publishing, 2012.

54 Chris Hadfield. *An Astronaut's Guide to Life on Earth: What Going to Space Taught Me About Ingenuity, Determination, and Being Prepared for Anything.* Little, Brown and Company, 2013.

55 Omar L. Harris. *Leader Board: The DNA of High Performance Teams.* The Pantheon Collective, 2018.

56 Patrick Lencioni. *The Five Dysfunctions of a Team: A Leadership Fable.* Jossey-Bass, 2003.

57 Donald O. Clifton and Markus Buckingham. *Now Discover Your Strengths: How to Develop Your Talents and Those of the People You Manage.* Simon & Schuster, 2004.

58 Travis Bradberry and Jean Greaves. *Emotional Intelligence 2.0.* TalentSmart, 2009.

59 Jack Welch with John A. Byrne. *Jack: Straight from the Gut.* Grand Central Publishing, 2003.

60 Jim Collins. *Great by Choice: Uncertainty, Chaos, and Luck—Why Some Thrive Despite Them All.* Harper Business, 2011.

61 Walter Isaacson. *Steve Jobs.* Simon & Schuster, 2011.

62 Patrick Lencioni. *The Ideal Team Player: How to Recognize and Cultivate the Three Essential Virtues.* Jossey-Bass, 2016.

63 John C. Maxwell. *The 17 Essential Qualities of a Team Player: Becoming the Kind of Person Every Team Wants.* Thomas Nelson, 2006.

64 Simon Sinek. *The Infinite Game.* Penguin Group, 2019.

65 Abraham Maslow. *Maslow on Management.* John Wiley & Sons, 1998.

66 Héctor García and Francesc Miralles. *Ikigai: The Japanese Secret to a Long and Happy Life.* Penguin Books, 2017.

67 Tom Rath. *Wellbeing: The Five Essential Elements.* Gallup Press, 2010.

68 Arianna Huffington. *Thrive: The Third Metric to Redefining Success and Creating a Life of Well-Being, Wisdom, and Wonder.* Random House, 2014.

Afterword

Writing this book was an unusual experience for me. I usually outline in depth, conduct copious reading and research, then handwrite until I achieve completion. In the past, this process has taken anywhere from twelve years, in the case of my novel *One Blood*, to two years for my last book, *Leader Board: The DNA of High Performance Teams*. However, in November 2019 something happened that locked my mind into focus. My mother was diagnosed with metastatic bile duct cancer: It was considered stage four and uncurable.

I was asleep on a plane from São Paulo, Brazil, to Charlotte, NC, near where my parents lived, to be with my family, when I awoke suddenly with an idea blazing in my mind. I needed to write about servant leadership. I needed to try to find a way to break through and connect with all the like-minded people in the world who are equally passionate about this issue.

My parents, like many of ours, have been models of servant leadership for my entire life. The thought that I might be losing my mother spurred me into action. I hastily texted the chapter headings into my phone's notes application and started writing the very next day. Everything was flowing smoothly until January 26, 2020. On that day, while at hospital and sitting at my mother's bedside, I learned that one of my basketball idols, Kobe Bryant, had died, along with his thirteen-year-old daughter Gianna and seven others.

Kobe and Gianna's death gave me a jolt. Life is too short to be unhappy and unfulfilled. Whatever you may make of Kobe's complicated legacy, what is undeniable about the man is that he knew his talents and worked his entire life to maximize his potential, while learning how to lead, serve, and inspire along the way. He was an example of an ego-driven 'me, me, me' star who grew to understand the power of partnership and service—first, as a player trying to maximize his team and, later and more importantly, as a father and self-proclaimed 'girldad.' He experienced periods of disengagement initially in his first few years in the NBA, and later after winning championships with Shaquille O'Neal, and again after suffering a rash of career-threatening injuries. But true to the personal effectiveness lessons in this book, he led by example, influencing everyone to follow his unique, uncompromising standard.

My father has been my life's best model of self-sacrifice, humility, and consistency. My mother invested copious hours during my childhood, helped me discover my unique talents and transform them into strengths. And as I grew into the leader I am today, I have been able to watch and learn from Kobe Bryant's pursuit of excellence in his field while making a ton of mistakes and attempting to boss his way to championships. It is not coincidental that it took Kobe's softened and personalized approach to teammates, and presenting a more authentic version of himself to the public, to achieve his ultimate goal of winning back-to-back championships as 'the man.' Ironically, by the time he achieved his two-peat, it was no longer about carrying a group to the title due to his individual strengths—it was about playing his role as part of a true team leader.

My ask of you reading this is to no longer settle for the status quo, especially if you are responsible for others as a team leader. Whatever your company culture may be, your people deserve better. They deserve to live more fulfilled lives. They deserve to feel engaged and productive at work. They deserve to have their talents understood and developed. They deserve to work for someone who is, first of all, a human being who sees and cares for their struggles and is invested in their success.

I don't know how much time my parents have on this Earth, but I know that I will dedicate the time left to serving them as a dedicated son. Kobe and Gianna have no time left, but you do. Accept and make no excuses for creating a life of which you—and those you love, and who love you—can be proud. Become a nurturer of others' success and watch your own success flourish. Make each day count, as you develop yourself and others in pursuit of your *ikigai* and version of self-actualization.

I am so grateful to you for investing your valuable time in reading this manifesto. You could have been reading anything, so the fact that you chose this title means the world to me. It also means, I hope, that we are like-minded and on the same mission. I will not stop fighting for the rights of employees around the world to live more fulfilled lives. It's a travesty that something we spend more than half of our life doing can bring us such misery, when it could be an infinite source of positivity, possibility, and progress.

Therefore, I am going to ask you for two last favors, dear reader. The first is to review this book on Amazon.com. The second is that you pass on this manifesto to as many of your colleagues as you think will actually read it.

This revolution is word-of-mouth, and hand-to-hand. I can't do it without your support, but together we truly can change the world.

Omar L. Harris
São Paulo, Brazil
February 13, 2020

Leader Board: The DNA of High Performance Teams

Review from the *US Daily Review:*

Leadership is an art, a discipline, and a skill well worth studying. And if you love books by leadership gurus such as Stephen Covey or Patrick Lencioni, you'll love *Leaderboard: The DNA of High Performance Teams* by Omar L. Harris. This handy book makes a compelling argument for rethinking how we hire our talent and lead our teams. A team is only as good as its manager—and this book shows managers how to completely transform their own ability to hire, lead and engage their teams.

Harris's enthusiasm for his subject is palpable, and he's certainly an expert. As an executive as well as a leadership coach, he combines his own experience in what works with modern leadership theories. Entrepreneurial by nature, Harris dove into the pharma industry as a rising star and quickly worked his way up the ranks. He clearly finds the corporate milieu, with its challenges and fast pace, a pleasure. He's lived and worked from Turkey to Brazil to Indonesia, for firms such as

Schering-Plough, Pfizer, and now, Allergen. His approach to leadership crosses cultures and geographies, which is vital to today's global economy.

The book is filled with utility. Harris has gathered a trove of the best advice from leadership gurus, and turned them into applicable tools. But he doesn't just repeat these theories, he builds on them—showing specifically the how and why of their effectiveness. The psychologist Bruce Tuckman's classic model of team growth—forming, storming, norming and performing—figures broadly: Harris illuminates how the progression contributes to organizational success.

He also debunks some of the theories we've all come to agree, including the edict to hire star talent. Instead of A players we need A teams, Harris asserts, and lays out a step-by-step strategy to building them. He's a big proponent of turning an interview into a kind of audition, packed with questions designed to reveal the strengths as well as weaknesses of prospects. There's a pragmatic, common-sense logic behind his approach: Many a book on leading great teams glosses over one essential requirement—you can't have great teams if you don't know how to hire great team players. *Leaderboard* fills that gap.

The book isn't just a series of charts or tables, though there are plenty of these. It's also the chronicle of a fictional executive, Sam Lombardi, who's about to launch a fast-paced campaign in his firm and needs everyone on board. Like many in high-pressure, high stakes managerial roles, Lombardi has to think on his feet as he tackles disengaged team members, recalcitrant colleagues, and endless challenges. Harris keeps the decision-making process transparent, and we see team-building happening in real time. It's a refreshing format that injects some old-fashioned storytelling into the read.

Harris' *Leaderboard* will help any leader, manager recruiter, people manager or HR pro revitalize their approach to leading and hiring. The book offers actionable steps, well-explained, useful theories, energetic language—Harris has fun creating his own terms, such as 'INNERviewing' each team member—and a relatable story. For anyone concerned with organizational culture, with engagement, with talent that fits, and with sparking better performance than ever before, this title should be on the shelf.

Foreword: Team DNA

I first encountered the concept of team formation in 2005 during a team-building workshop. I was struck by how much sense it made. Teams formed, stormed, normed, and performed. A nice, linear model. Functional.

It was in sophomore biology that I first learned about proteins, RNA, DNA, and genes. I was amazed at how such complexity could emerge from a single cell and how information, form, and function passed vertically from generation to generation. Simplistically, a gene encodes a message to build a protein, therefore enabling information to perform a function. Linear and also functional.

Teams, like genes, exist to perform a function, the success of which results in the achievement (or not) of a given goal. There are a whole host of chemical and biological processes to ensure the proper functioning of genes, but what of the role of the team leaders—the true catalysts of proper team function in the business world? The idea of how to best influence and accelerate team formation and performance has fascinated me ever since I joined my first corporation back in 1998 and continued as I matriculated from individual contributor to team member to enterprise leader. After years of researching and experimentation in the real world, I believe every leader can learn how to effectively accelerate the team-building process and dramatically increase its speed to achieve faster results.

The team-building process was coined by psychologist Bruce Tuckman in his 1965 article, 'Developmental Sequence in Small Groups.' Tuckman defined the first stage as related to 'orientation to the task [known as forming], in which group members attempt to identify the task in terms of its relevant parameters and the way the group experience will be used to accomplish the task. The group must decide upon the type of information they will need in dealing with the task and how this information is to be obtained.' He continued:

The second phase in the development of group structure is labeled as intragroup conflict [storming]. Group members become hostile toward one another and toward a leader as a means of expressing their individuality and resisting the formation of group structure. Interaction is uneven and 'infighting' is common. The lack of unity is an outstanding feature of this phase. There are characteristic key issues that polarize the group and boil down to the conflict over progression into the 'unknown' of interpersonal relations or regression to the security of earlier dependence[...]

The third group structure phase is labeled as the development of group cohesion [norming]. Group members accept the group and accept the idiosyncrasies of fellow members. The group becomes an entity by virtue of its acceptance by the members, their desire to maintain and perpetuate it, and the establishment of new group-generated norms to insure the group's existence. Harmony is of maximum importance, and task conflicts are avoided to ensure harmony[...]

The fourth and final developmental phase of group structure is labeled as functional role-relatedness [performing]. The group, which was established as an entity during the preceding phase, can now become a problem-solving instrument. It does this by directing itself to members as objects, since the subjective relationship between members has already been established. Members can now adopt and play roles that will enhance the task activities of the group, since they have learned to relate to one another as social entities in the preceding stage. Role structure is not an issue but an instrument which can now be directed at the task. The group becomes a 'sounding board' off which the task is 'played.'

Over the years, I have found that there is a strong correlation between a leader's dedication, focus, and skill in moving his or her team through these four stages and the speed with which the team achieves desired results. I have also found that it can be difficult to connect the dots between advice from leadership gurus and the application of their guidance in the real world. Therefore, I dedicated myself to the task of developing and testing a simple process you can now apply to successfully navigating your teams from forming to performing.

Leader Board: The DNA of High-Performance Teams is a resource that any leader can use to fast-track team development. Consider *Leader Board* a two-for-one inspiration from the best business minds of the last twenty years combined with an innovative system that puts their ideas and practical experiences to work in the form of Team Performance Acceleration Principles (TPAPs). In the pages that follow, you will be immersed and 'edutained' by the fictional story of a leader trying to do something very special with a group of people he is leading. By investing in this story, you will take away actionable wisdom that has been successfully applied in the real world with teams of all sizes, in many different countries and cultural contexts.

Specifically, from this book you will take away four completely new tools that I use to navigate every team I lead toward high performance.

- W.H.O.M. is an acronym that stands for work-ethic, heart, optimism, and maturity—the basic building blocks I require in every team member I hire. Hopefully, you will find the thirty-two W.H.O.M. interview questions as useful as I have as starting points in ensuring you source the right attributes in your key hires.

- As your team is being constructed, INNERviewing is an important step in defining your team's why based on the individual journeys, needs, motivations, and demotivators of each person. By aligning each person's why with the team's objective, you will gain trust and inspire the collective to be more than the sum of the parts.

- Once the why is clear, building the team's Leader Board defines how you can more effectively work together. A Leader Board demonstrates who your team leaders should be in terms of getting things done, advocating and elevating standards, ensuring effective ways of working, and solving problems. It will help break down silos and drive greater accountability and productivity. You will find it easy to assemble and activate your own team's DNA via this approach.

- And finally, the fifteen Team Performance Acceleration Principles (TPAPs) presented in the discussion section of this book will permit you to meet your team where they are on the journey from forming to performing. Then, you'll learn to masterfully steer your group through the stages faster than ever before.

Every leader can learn how to tap into and unlock their team's DNA to achieve breakout results. Now there is a simple and actionable approach to accelerating teams through the four stages of development: forming, storming, norming, and performing. This approach comes alive through the narrative presented in *Leader Board*. Please enjoy the story and stay for the discussion section, where we will delve specifically into the Team Performance Acceleration Principles (TPAPs), with actionable takeaways and resources you can immediately begin applying with your own teams.

About the Author

Omar L. Harris hails from Pittsburgh, PA, and is passionate about leading teams, high-performance coaching, and inspiring the future leaders of today and tomorrow.

He is a Gallup Certified Strengths coach, bestselling and award-winning author, independent publishing guru, entrepreneur, and twenty-year veteran of the global pharmaceutical industry, with stints at Pfizer, Schering-Plough, Merck, GSK, and Allergan, while living in the U.S., Brazil, the Middle East, and Southeast Asia.

He is the author of three other books: *One Blood* (under the pseudonym Qwantu Amaru), *From Authors to Entrepreneurs* (with co-authors Stephanie Casher and James W. Lewis), and *Leader Board: The DNA of High-Performance Teams*.

Omar is active on social media: Join his mailing list and/or follow him at his personal website, or on LinkedIn, Facebook, Twitter, and Instagram.

www.omarlharris.com
www.twitter.com/strengthsleader
www.facebook.com/authorleadercoach
www.linkedin.com/in/omarlharris

Subscribe to his newsletter: www.omarlharris.com/members